ETHNICITY, DISABILITY AND CHRONIC ILLNESS

'RACE', HEALTH AND SOCIAL CARE

Series editors:

Professor Waqar I.U. Ahmad, Professor of Primary Care Research and Director, Centre for Research in Primary Care, University of Leeds.

Professor Charles Husband, Professor of Social Analysis and Director, Ethnicity and Social Policy Research Unit (ESPR), University of Bradford.

Minority ethnic groups now constitute over 5 per cent of the UK population. While research literature has mushroomed on the one hand in 'race' and ethnic relations generally, and on the other in clinical and epidemiological studies of differences in conditions and use of health and social services, there remains a dearth of credible social scientific literature on the health and social care of minority ethnic communities. Social researchers have hitherto largely neglected issues of 'race' and ethnicity, while acknowledging the importance of gender, class and, more recently, (dis)ability in both the construction of and provision for health and social care needs. Consequently the available social science texts on health and social care largely reflect the experiences of the white population and have been criticized for marginalizing minority ethnic people.

This series aims to provide an authoritative source of policy relevant texts which specifically address issues of health and social care in contemporary multi-ethnic Britain. Given the rate of change in the structure of health and social care services, demography and the political context of state welfare, there is a need for a critical appraisal of the health and social care needs of, and provision for, the minority ethnic communities in Britain. By the nature of the issues we shall address, this series will draw upon a wide range of professional and academic expertise, thus enabling a deliberate and necessary integration of theory and practice in these fields. The books will be inter-disciplinary and written in clear, non-technical language which will appeal to a broad range of students, academic and professionals with a common interest in 'race', health and social care.

Current and forthcoming titles
Waqar I.U. Ahmad: *Ethnicity, Disability and Chronic Illness*
Waqar I.U. Ahmad and Karl Atkin: *'Race' and Community Care*
Elizabeth Anionwu and Karl Atkin: *The Politics of Sickle Cell and Thalassaemia – 20 Years On*
Kate Gerrish, Charles Husband and Jennifer Mackenzie: *Nursing for a Multi-ethnic Society*
Savita Katbamna: *'Race' and Childbirth*
Derek Kirton: *'Race', Ethnicity and Adoption*
Lena Robinson: *'Race', Communication and the Caring Professions*

ETHNICITY, DISABILITY AND CHRONIC ILLNESS

Edited by
Waqar I.U. Ahmad

Open University Press
Buckingham · Philadelphia

For
Ammi Ji

Open University Press
Celtic Court
22 Ballmoor
Buckingham
MK18 1XW

e-mail: enquiries@openup.co.uk
world wide web: http://www.openup.co.uk

and
325 Chestnut Street
Philadelphia, PA 19106, USA

First Published 2000

A catalogue record of this book is available from the British Library

ISBN   0 335 19982 8 (pb)   0 335 19983 6 (hb)

Library of Congress Cataloging-in-Publication Data
Ethnicity, disability, and chronic illness / edited by Waqar I.U. Ahmad.
    p.   cm. – (Race, health, and social care)
  Includes bibliographical references and index.
  ISBN 0-335-19983-6 (hb). – ISBN 0-335-19982-8 (pbk.)
  1. Handicapped – Medical care – Great Britain.   2. Minorities – Medical care – Great Britain.   3. Chronically ill – Medical care – Great Britain.   I. Ahmad, W. I.U. (Waqar Ihsan-Ullah), 1957– II. Series.
RA485.E854   2000
362.1'089'00941–dc21   99–41465
                                                              CIP

Typeset by Graphicraft Limited, Hong Kong
Printed in Great Britain by Biddles Ltd, Guildford and King's Lynn

Contents

Notes on contributors

Waqar I.U. Ahmad* is Professor of Primary Care Research and Director, Centre for Research in Primary Care, University of Leeds.

Elizabeth N. Anionwu is Dean of Nursing at Wolfson Institute of Health Sciences, Thames Valley University.

Karl Atkin* is Principal Research Fellow at the Centre for Research in Primary Care, University of Leeds.

Padma Bhakta is a Research Associate at the Nuffield Community Care Studies Unit, University of Leicester.

Rampaul Chamba* was a Research Fellow at the University of Bradford and is now a doctoral student at the University of California, San Diego.

Aliya Darr* was a Research Fellow at the School of Healthcare Studies, University of Bradford, and is now at the Centre for Research in Primary Care, University of Leeds.

Lesley Jones* is a Senior Research Fellow at the Centre for Research in Primary Care, University of Leeds.

Savita Katbamna is a Research Associate at the Nuffield Community Care Studies Unit, University of Leicester.

Gillian Parker is Nuffield Professor of Community Care and Director of the Nuffield Community Care Studies Unit, University of Leicester.

* All these authors were at the Ethnicity and Social Policy Research Unit, University of Bradford, when the research studies reported here were undertaken.

1

Introduction

Waqar I.U. Ahmad

Analyses of health and health care of minority ethnic groups constitute a major industry. However, interest in disability and chronic illness among minority ethnic communities is relatively new. Much of this research is small scale; often it lacks theoretical sophistication. The more voluminous and more sophisticated mainstream literature on disability, chronic illness and caring rarely includes minority groups. Debates on ethnicity, disability, caring and chronic illness usually occupy different discourses and politics. This book aims to make a contribution to both theoretical and policy debates in these areas. It does so by bringing together issues, debates and politics rarely discussed under the same cover.

The debates in the fields covered by this book are complex and contingent. To begin with, notions of impairment and disability themselves lack precision. Impairment is defined as an imperfection or loss of function of an organ or limb. Disability refers to the stigma attached to individuals who have impairments and the consequent marginalization and discrimination experienced by people with impairments (Oliver 1990; Swain *et al.* 1993). The fundamental argument is that the disability resides in the workings of an unjust society; a more inclusive environment ranging from inclusive employment, education and transport policies would allow people with impairments to perform their roles as citizens. Citizenship, as for those without impairments, combines responsibilities towards the society and the state, with social and political rights of the individual. As a model for conceptualizing the discrimination experienced by people with impairments, the social model of disability is powerful and necessary. Reconceptualizing disability as a social issue rather than a personal tragedy is necessary to ensure that the disablist marginalization experienced by people with impairments is seen in similar terms to racist, homophobic or sexist discrimination, that is discrimination experienced by a whole class of people (with impairments) which systematically disadvantages them compared to the mainstream of society. The loss of independence, lack of control over resources, the marginalization of personal voice in decisions about personal care, relationships, lifestyle and tasks of daily living are all important markers of experiencing disability.

However, the social model of disability requires a number of qualifications. For many the distinction between impairment and disability remains problematic. The form and severity of impairment have an impact on whether someone experiences disabling consequences. The time of onset of impairment and its severity have distinct consequences for people and their identity. For example, the mobilization around British Sign Language by Deaf people is not shared by many who become deaf in older age or due to an accident. My relatively modest visual impairment is easily corrected by wearing spectacles and would not be regarded as disabling; that is, I do not experience any perceptible stigma or marginalization because of this minor impairment. Many conditions leading to impairments require ongoing medical interventions or make the impaired person dependent on medical technology for survival. Indeed, for some conditions, such as asthma, medicines can help control the symptoms and thus help reduce the stigma and discrimination experienced by the affected individual (Prout *et al.* 1999; see also later discussion of sickle cell disorders in Chapters 4 and 7).

Political movements, almost by definition, are historically and culturally specific. Thus some of the arguments about loss of control or independence in relation to the social model of disability may seem over-westernized to many for whom interdependence, mutual support and reciprocity are the hallmarks of social and family relationships. This is not to trivialize the discrimination experienced by disabled people within Asian or other non-western societies. The disabled individuals do still experience oppression and marginalization, but their marginalization can be understood only against what is considered 'normal' for someone of their gender, age and class in their own cultures. Normalcy is not a given universal; thus impairments require to be seen in their social and cultural context. The discrimination experienced by minority ethnic people in their own ethnic communities may lead to the lack of an ability to reciprocate, to engage in equal or incremental social or economic exchange, or fulfil other obligations normal for their non-disabled siblings. The stigma of impairment, as in the west, may lead to social isolation, infantilization or 'invisibility' – in Finklestein's terms 'social death' (Finklestein 1993). Minority ethnic communities live within not only their own social structures but also the structures of the wider society. Some normative values (facilitative or oppressive) may be difficult to fulfil because of their minority status within Britain. This range of issues requires an assessment of impairment and disability among minority ethnic people both in the context of their cultures and their minority status.

I have noted that many of the debates pursued in this volume utilize different discourses; often they are conducted in opposition to each other. For example, the debates on carers and disabled persons are often presented as binary opposites. Both the disability movement and carers' organizations have fuelled this notional opposition. Disabled people have sometimes portrayed carers as oppressive and colluding with professionals to undermine disabled people's rights to self-determination. On the other hand, literature on carers, developed from feminist critiques of the gendered nature of domestic labour, understandably highlighted the 'labour' and 'burdens' of care. These constructs were somewhat uncritically reproduced in research work on carers. The recent emphasis on so-called 'young carers' is perhaps particularly problematic for its denial of disabled people's parental contribution and young people's contributions to family well-being in families without disabled parents. Arguments about the distinctiveness of being a carer or disabled person have become ossified in an essentialist identity politics fuelled by state welfare policies. Here, carers' representatives highlight the burdens on them from the failure of the state to provide adequate support to families. And disabled people emphasize their unnecessary dependence on the family because the state marginalizes disabled people from education, economy and other spheres of life.

However, some recent work demonstrates the symbiotic relationship between carers and disabled people (e.g. G. Parker 1993b), emphasizing interdependence and reciprocity rather than the assumed one-way relationship of disabled people always receiving and never providing care. That disabled people do not stop functioning in their own capacity as parents or family members, and thus stop caring for or about others is also noted. The relationship is especially complex when it comes to dealing with disabled people from minority ethnic groups and disabled children. For disabled children, parents are the greatest allies and confront society and services to ensure the best for them. The stigma associated with impairment is often shared by other family members, although the parents and extended families may themselves have disablist attitudes. For minority ethnic disabled people, own families and communities provide vital buffers against a racist society. Perhaps there is a greater tendency for the stigma of impairment to be shared among the family members within the often more communally oriented South Asian communities. Having a disabled family member, for example, may affect the marriage chances of siblings or the social standing of the family. The disablism within the minority ethnic groups is as pernicious as in the white society and must be challenged; but the importance of alliances with their own families and ethnic communities in struggles against racial oppression cannot be overemphasized (Begum *et al.* 1994; M. Hill 1994; Stuart 1996).

Many minority ethnic disabled people involved in the disabled people's movement experience racist marginalization (M. Hill 1994; see also Ahmad *et al.* 1998). Millie Hill (1994) noted this marginalization:

Black Disabled people have often found that they are regularly forced to negate the issue of their race in order to 'fit in with' the rest of the Disability Movement. Alternatively, they are compelled to face the ire of white Disabled people when, no longer content with having to lop

of huge chunks of their identity in order to be 'allowed in', they go off
and set up their own associations. As one Black Disabled person said
'they always talk of brotherhood but they are not really our brothers'.

(M. Hill 1994: 74–9)

That the disabled people's movement fears recognizing or responding to
diversity is not surprising. Parallel journeys have been undertaken within
the feminist movement (Carby 1982) and the anti-racist movement (Modood
1994). In the feminist movement, for example, black feminists were critical
of racism within feminism and while recognizing the sexism of their own
communities, argued for alliances with black men to fight racism. Millie
Hill (1994) put forward a similar argument in relation to disabled people's
movement and the need for 'black' disabled people to build alliances with
the black communities in order to fight racism. In anti-racism, the recognition of religious or cultural diversity was feared to dilute the collective
struggles against racist discrimination. Yet many felt that the collective
struggle should not require cultural and religious identities to be sacrificed.
The inability of the anti-racist movement to deal with struggles for religious
respect raised questions of its relevance to those who claimed to experience
more discrimination on the bases of religion or culture, rather than necessarily colour. Movements and discourses which do not accommodate obvious diversity risk becoming irrelevant. Yet the fear of fragmentation through
ever increasing sub-identities are very real; often such fragmentation is fuelled
by the opponents of these movements.

The politics of organization against different oppressions do not necessarily overlap. The social models of disability, on the one hand, and of
deafness, on the other, share many common fundamentals, for example,
arguments about marginalization and discrimination by an uncaring and
oppressive mainstream society. However, their analyses and solutions are
often very different. Whereas the disabled people's movement, quite rightly,
argues against segregation – a vehicle of oppression and of 'social death' for
so long – segregated education is strongly argued by many deaf people. For
the latter, a shared culture and language in schools for deaf children allows
them to develop strong identities, progress educationally and acquire important life skills. Deafness, so goes the argument, is not an 'impairment'; deaf
people are disabled by a hearing society's failure to communicate with deaf
people through a language that Deaf people are skilled in using. Deaf people
are thus a linguistic minority; for some – perhaps stretching a point – they
are a distinct 'ethnic group' with a unique culture, history and language. Of
course, these arguments are not without problem, and among the challenges
to this conceptualization of a universal Deaf culture, are those from minority
ethnic deaf people. We return to this in Chapter 5.

The literatures on disability and chronic illness occupy somewhat distinct
spheres, both theoretically and politically. Yet disability and chronic illness
often go hand in hand and show some overlap in terms of consequences
and discourses. Many impairments are progressive or episodic, or directly

related to the effects of a chronic condition. For many chronic conditions, the impact on personal biography, lifestyles and identities is not dissimilar to that of relatively stable impairments. Stigma and discrimination are also shared. Disruptions to identities may also be shared between people who become chronically ill or have impairments later in life. However, the relationship with medicine is often quite different. In many chronic conditions, escape from the medical model may not be desired or possible, or at best may be transitory. The use of medicine to control pain, or to halt or minimize the damage or life-threatening consequences of illness is not uncommon. Indeed, as Prout *et al.* (1999) note, medicine may be used to maintain a sense of normalcy and thus minimize stigma and marginalization. In sickle cell disorders and thalassaemia major, two major chronic conditions affecting predominantly minority ethnic groups in Britain, the link between chronic illness and disability become closely tied. Both are inherited impairments of the haemoglobin. In thalassaemia major, for example, the affected individual does not make enough haemoglobin and thus requires monthly transfusions for life. An important side-effect of transfusions is excess iron, which needs nightly injections of an agent commonly known as desferal in order to be excreted. Complications of thalassaemia can range from failure to enter puberty, restricted growth and damage to various organs, to premature death. The condition is very much technology dependent; rejection of the personalized medical model is not an option; compliance with medical regimens is a condition of continued life and of maintaining some control over the condition. In order to reduce the impairments relating to the condition, and to limit the stigma attached to many of the impairments, compliance with the medical regimes is a necessity. Not only are chronic illness, impairments and disability closely related, but also the discourses on the social and medical models of disability are closely related in case of thalassaemia. The reliance on medical interventions to maintain life and improve quality of life need not be seen in opposition to struggles for dignity and inclusion within a society which discriminates against disabled and chronically ill people and their families.

Finally, minority ethnic groups, disabled people and carers, as distinct groups have criticized the state and welfare services for not recognizing their needs, locating their needs in their own presumed failings and placing barriers in their access to substantive citizenship. For minority ethnic disabled people and carers these barriers are even greater, including questions about their citizenship rights, unwillingness of services to reach out to non-speakers of English, the use of stereotypes of 'caring extended families', arguments about 'low numbers' to marginalize needs, and keeping users and carers ignorant of their rights. In a recently published national study of minority ethnic parents with severely disabled children, a consistent picture of greater disadvantage is presented (Chamba *et al.* 1999). Parents with severely disabled children tend to be poorer compared to the general population. Minority ethnic parents with severely disabled children consistently faced greater adversity suggesting that their ethnic minority status was important in explaining their greater poverty, lack of service provision and access to benefits.

About the book

The contributors to this book are among the leading researchers in the field of ethnicity, disability, chronic illness and caring. The chapters were specially commissioned to provide a coherent package of previously unpublished material based on major research projects. Contributions cover three important but overlapping areas with chapters complementing each other. Chapters 2 and 3 explore how disability or chronic illness is conceptualized and the implications of particular definitions for disabled people and carers. Chapters 4 and 5 focus on living with a disability or chronic illness. The final three chapters engage with the role of services in providing support to disabled people and carers. A brief theoretical and policy context for the chapters is provided below; this demonstrates the complex and contingent nature of debates addressed in this book and relates the chapters to the substantive debates introduced above.

In Chapter 2, Savita Katbamna, Padma Bhakta and Gillian Parker explore perceptions of disability and care-giving relationships among South Asian communities. Their findings are based on the first major survey of Asian carers (and some disabled people). Not surprisingly, they note that like the general population, the South Asian communities carry disablist attitudes which affect disabled people and their families alike. Many parallels with the attitudes of the general population are noted. Impairments carry social stigma. Disabled individuals and their families confront negative comments and social isolation from some relatives. Disabled relatives were often treated as invisible; in social relationships with the family, people excluded the disabled individual. As a father comments to Katbamna and colleagues: 'They ask about the other kids but they don't ask about the one who's disabled . . . Isn't he a human being as well?'

Carers were concerned about the disabled relative maintaining a stake in society and having a viable social role. Caring was done out of love and affection but the caring responsibilities were gendered, with the female moral identity closely tied to the caring role. Consequently, male carers not only were thought to be deserving of greater support but also experienced ridicule for carrying out tasks associated with the 'female' gender role. Not all carers saw the caring role as one sided; the reciprocity within the relationship was important for many and was conceptualized either in the present sense or in a historical sense. Caring for a disabled relative impacts on other family members, not only in terms of having social, emotional and financial consequences but also in terms of chances of finding marriage partners. For some (especially Hindus and Sikhs), association of disability with notions of retribution for past sins created numerous problems. As noted, many of these carers' experiences are similar to those of white carers.

However, there are some important differences. These carers often care in greater isolation, with little information about the disabled relative's condition, or about support available for the disabled relative or themselves. Importantly, many faced criticism from wider family and community if they approached services for help, this being regarded as a sign of not being able to cope or of abdicating responsibility to care and thus damaging their moral identity as a 'good' wife, daughter-in-law or son. There was only limited support from the extended families. The account provided by Katbamna and colleagues demonstrates the inextricable connectedness of disabled people and their family members, making the often promoted binary opposition between disabled people and carers unviable.

As Katbamna and colleagues note, perceptions of disability and care-giving relationships matter. Perceptions of impairment, however, do not develop in a social or historical vacuum. Societal views of impairment and of disabled people rest on assumptions both about normality, and values attached to being able to perform certain tasks in relation to age, gender and culture. By and large, the limitations experienced by disabled people are thought to reside in their impairment rather than in the disablist assumptions and structures of the wider society. Professionals play an important part in constructing notions of normalcy. In particular, the medical profession has played an important, though far from honourable, part in constructions of women, disabled people and non-white people. Medicine's legitimization of contemporary discourses and practices of oppression has been much criticized (Doyal and Pennel 1979; Littlewood and Lipsedge 1989; Oliver 1990; Ahmad 1993). Waqar Ahmad, Karl Atkin and Rampaul Chamba have researched in the areas of disability, deafness and haemoglobin disorders. In Chapter 3, they explore attribution of 'cause' for haemoglobin disorders and deafness by professionals and parents. Ahmad (1994) has argued that historically, racialized minority groups have been thought in the west to be dangerous to their own health. Their cultures, lifestyles and genetic make-up have all been criticized for their presumed intellectual backwardness, ill-health and premature deaths. Consanguinity, the practice of marrying within one's own kin-group, has recently emerged as a powerful discourse, combining fears about diseased genes and inferior cultures. Ahmad and colleagues note that professionals overemphasized the role of consanguinity in 'explaining' the child's condition, and the discourse on consanguinity was based less on clinical evidence but more on racist discourses on undesirability of Asian family forms, presumed oppression of Asian women, and the desirability of adopting the British way of life. The unhelpful emphasis on consanguinity meant that parents often remained uninformed about the genetic basis of their child's condition, and lacked information necessary to care adequately for the child. Parents resented the emphasis on consanguinity; this emphasis damaged professionals' relationships with parents, engendered feelings of guilt in parents and, at times, undermined their ability to come to terms with the diagnosis. At the same time, some parents internalized the professional discourse linking consanguinity to their child's condition, an internalization that they found unhelpful and often contradictory. Chapter 3 provides a powerful case study in the marriage of diverse oppressive discourses, all predicated on assumptions of alienness and inferiority of these families, their cultures and genes 'causing havoc to their children'. Regrettably, the history of professionals too often being part of the problem facing minority ethnic users is repeated in these accounts. However, the chapter also shows challenges to oppressive discourses both from parents and from some professionals.

Chapters 4 and 5 focus on living with an impairment or chronic illness. In Chapter 4, Karl Atkin and Waqar Ahmad present findings from a qualitative study of young people with sickle cell disorder. (The study also included young people with thalassaemia major but this is not reported here.) Sickle cell disorder is an inherited disorder of the haemoglobin, resulting in the characteristic 'painful crisis', and often leading to damage to vital organs and thus secondary impairments; it can be life threatening. Its association with people of African descent gives it a racialized character. Its neglect by the National Health Service (NHS) is often located by the affected people in it being a 'black disease'. Chapter 4 explores the experiences of young affected people in relation to medical precautions, treatment and lifestyles. Sickle cell disorder (SCD) is episodic and variable, making medical prognosis difficult and allowing affected people and their families greater scope to maintain alternative constructions of the condition, constructions which emphasize their normality and where an undermining of medical discourse in itself is an important coping mechanism (see S.A. Hill 1994). Precautions suggested by health professionals thus carry less weight than for other more or consistently technology dependent conditions where the effects of non-compliance are immediate. With SCD, consequences of non-adherence to medical and lifestyle precautions are both unpredictable and temporally distanced. Yet during the painful crisis, the reversion to the medical model is inevitable and thus alternative constructions of SCD remain vulnerable. The relationship of SCD to personal identity and strategies to maintain a positive self-image and control over one's life are explored by Atkin and Ahmad. They note that impairments or ill-health are not experienced in a social vacuum; in relation to SCD and young people, age, gender, ethnicity, family relationships and lifestyle choices are all important. These young people's experiences of living with SCD can be made sense of only against this wider context.

Maintaining a focus on identity and impairments, Waqar Ahmad, Aliya Darr and Lesley Jones in Chapter 5 discuss minority ethnic deaf people. As noted, the Deaf people's movement constructs deafness as linguistic oppression by an unsympathetic hearing world. The unity of Deaf people and claims to having an independent Deaf culture help sustain this image of being a linguistic minority, separate both from the hearing world and from the disabled people. As in the disability movement and anti-racism, the shared experience of (language) oppression is privileged over ethnic or religious diversity among Deaf people; it also helps maintain distance from the disabled people's movement. It is this conception of a Deaf culture in which very many South Asian and African Caribbean Deaf people were socialized. However, as Chapter 5 (based on a national study of minority ethnic deaf people – Ahmad *et al.* 1998) shows, the acquisition and maintenance of a Deaf identity was often at the expense of ethnic and religious identities. Minority ethnic deaf people experienced marginalization from their ethnic and religious communities because of language barriers. Their easier access to the predominantly white Deaf culture made alliances with white Deaf people easier. Yet they experienced racist marginalization within the white Deaf society. Ahmad and colleagues discuss the recent developments in self-organization of minority ethnic Deaf people around cultural and religious identities, a new-found pride in owning and celebrating their ethnicity and religion while maintaining a strong Deaf identity. The experiences of minority ethnic Deaf people mirror those of 'black' feminists (Carby 1982) and black disabled people (M. Hill 1994). The alliances with the Deaf community remain important but the racist marginalization shows the lack of acceptance of minority ethnic Deaf people by the white Deaf movement. Ethnic and religious communities remain important in giving Deaf people a sense of belonging and identity, and yet continue to 'disable' Deaf people, by their failure to learn to communicate with and continued negative attitudes towards Deaf people.

As noted earlier, substantive citizenship rights are often denied to minority ethnic groups as they are to disabled people. The tools of denial are varied and many, and discourses of 'race' and nation, deployed to undermine citizenship rights, go hand in hand with stereotypes of supportive extended families, used to deny needs for state welfare. The non-recognition of need and the unwillingness of agencies to provide services which are appropriate and accessible need to be considered against these twin contexts. The final three chapters explore minority ethnic users' interaction with state services.

In Chapter 6, Rampaul Chamba and Waqar Ahmad report some findings from the first major national survey of minority ethnic families of severely disabled children. With colleagues (Chamba *et al.* 1999), they collected data on nearly 600 South Asian and African Caribbean families who had one or more severely disabled children. Their work showed that compared to white families with severely disabled children, there was an added depth and intensity to the problems faced by minority ethnic families. A major problem faced by families is in relation to communication and information. In Chapter 6, Chamba and Ahmad note problems faced by non-users of English, many of whom still rely on informal interpreters; those provided with professional interpreters often find them less than ideal. Information about the condition and about services for the disabled person and the family is a vital resource for both disabled people and their families. This chapter shows that parents remained poorly informed about their child's condition but particularly about support available for the child and themselves.

Knowledge about and use of support groups remained poor and many parents had a variety of unmet needs for themselves and their children. Within the context of poverty, lack of access to benefits and barriers to services, the importance of professionals functioning as a resource for families cannot be overstated. Chamba *et al.* (1999), however, note that the variety and strength of barriers faced by minority ethnic parents of severely disabled children act to exclude them from society, leaving too many families 'living on the edge'. This work is important in that it provides numerical data to back up the increasing qualitative evidence on the poverty of service response to the needs of minority ethnic disabled and chronically ill people, and their families.

Earlier, Chapter 3 focused on young people's own accounts of living with SCD and demonstrated the symbiotic relationship between young people and their families. Chapter 7, concerned with the perspectives of parents whose children have sickle cell disorder or thalassaemia major, underlines the importance of this relationship both for the affected individual and the family. The personal and clinical consequences of SCD are noted above. Thalassaemia has the same pattern of inheritance as SCD but affected individuals are more technologically dependent and the condition is more stable. Services for these haemoglobin disorders remain patchy in coverage, quality and organization. Karl Atkin and Waqar Ahmad have been researching this field for some time (Ahmad and Atkin 1996a; Atkin and Ahmad 1998; Atkin *et al.* 1998a, 1998b) and here provide an account of parental experiences of using services. Confirming Chamba and Ahmad's (Chapter 6) findings, they note problems in information and service co-ordination, non-recognition of parental or children's needs, and limited language support for non-users of English. Especially importantly, they note variable and often very limited knowledge of the conditions among health professionals. This ignorance was often coupled with arrogance on the part of professionals, who discounted the considerable expertise of the affected children and their parents in relation to the condition. Affected children and their parents persevered with inadequate and unsympathetic care while, from considerable previous experience, knowing the shape and benefits of appropriate care. Not surprisingly, parents distrusted many health professionals. This led to sometimes strained relationships, and in particular made stays in hospital stressful for both the children and their parents. Within the general context of poor services and unhelpful practitioners, they also note the much appreciated facilitative role of specialist haemoglobinopathy workers. These workers occupied a central coordination role for parents, provided accessible information and support, were flexible and usually shared the users' cultural and linguistic background. Importantly, their performance shows how services can underwrite parental resources and support families and affected children through often trying times.

The problems of coordinating services within health care and across health and social care boundaries have been recognized for some time. Coordination becomes especially problematic when dealing with users requiring complex care packages needing multi-professional and multi-agency involvement. Problems experienced by disabled children and adults, and their families are noted by a number of researchers (Baldwin and Carlisle 1994; Twigg and Atkin 1994). The concept of a primary health care team was developed to provide, in the words of Padma Bhakta, Savita Katbamna and Gillian Parker (Chapter 8), 'a comprehensive pattern of services embracing social, psychological as well as physical needs'. Literature on the support needs of Asian carers is scant. Bhakta and colleagues' chapter is based on a significant research project on South Asian carers' needs and the role of primary health care teams. Here they focus on carers' experiences of using primary health care teams. They note that these teams can be supportive and facilitative; indeed some carers found them very helpful. However, they argue that for most carers, primary health care teams remained unhelpful. Consultations with general practitioners and other team members remained problematic. Professionals expressed negative attitudes towards carers and rarely appreciated the carers' role; their concerns about the disabled relative and the difficulties they experienced as carers were ignored. And carers remained poorly informed about the role of different team members. The chapter shows that the potential of primary health care teams being a key resource to carers remains to be realized, perhaps particularly so in relation to South Asian carers.

This book aims to add to the emerging literature in these fields. In theoretical terms it problematizes distinctions between users and carers, between the social model of disability and more individual medical discourses, and argues that chronic ill-health and impairment can be made sense of only within people's personal, social and citizenship contexts. Ethnicity and racism remain important aspects of this wider context for minority ethnic people with impairments or chronic ill-health, and their families; however, neither racism nor ethnic culture deterministically structure their attitudes or experiences. In terms of policy and practice the book highlights the continued problems experienced by minority ethnic disabled and chronically ill people and their families. Although many of these users' experiences are shared with white users, the intensity and persistence of disadvantage that minority ethnic users face can be understood only with reference to their racialized worlds.

Acknowledgements

My thanks to Karl Atkin for helpful comments on an earlier draft.

2

Perceptions of disability and care-giving relationships in South Asian communities

Savita Katbamna, Padma Bhakta and Gillian Parker

This chapter focuses on attitudes to disability, independence and care-giving relationships from the perspective of carers within British South Asian communities. The way that disability is defined and the meanings and values attached to it can have a major impact on the lives of disabled people and their carers. While there is some descriptive literature on minority ethnic carers' experiences of care-giving (Bould 1990; McCalman 1990), very few studies have explored in depth the meaning of disability to carers, the attitudes of carers towards disability, and the nature of their relationships with the persons being cared for (Fatimilehin and Nadirshaw 1994; Chamba *et al.* 1998b; Atkin and Ahmad 2000). Debates on dependence and independence in relation to disability and caring, as defined in the west, may not always be applicable to South Asian communities. The paucity of literature on this subject is matched by a similar dearth of literature on how disabled people within minority ethnic communities perceive their disability. The few studies in this area are limited to small-scale local surveys of elderly people (Bhalla and Blakemore 1981; Fenton 1987), surveys of young disabled adults and children (Confederation of Indian Organisations 1987; Begum 1992; Shah 1992) and the nature of the relationship they have with their carers (Begum 1992).

This is in marked contrast to the volume of literature which has examined the attitudes of white carers towards disability and the care-giving relationship (Lewis and Meredith 1988; Opie 1992; Beresford 1994a, 1994b; Lamb and Layzell 1995). Other studies (Qureshi and Walker 1989; G. Parker 1993a; 1993b) have explored disability and the care-giving relationship from the perspectives of both disabled persons and their carers. There is also a large literature documenting the experiences of disabled people within the white community (Ford and Sinclaire 1987; Morris 1989; Walmsley 1993; Lamb and Layzell 1994). In the 1990s, disabled writers

Table 2.1 Focus group and in-depth interview sample

	Male	Female	Total
Focus groups	27	59	86
In-depth interviews	12	22	34
Carers from focus groups interviewed in-depth	6	9	15
New carers interviewed in-depth	6	13	19
Total number of carers involved	33	72	105

Note: The findings presented here are based on the analysis of transcripts of focus group discussions and in-depth interviews

and commentators transformed academic writing and analysis of the politics of disability and of society's treatment of disabled people (Lonsdale 1990; Oliver 1990; Swain *et al.* 1993).

The study

The accounts presented in this chapter were collected for a major study on informal or family carers within the four main British South Asian communities: Punjabi Sikh, Gujarati Hindu and Bangladeshi and Pakistani Muslim (Katbamna and Bhakta 1998). Carers who took part in the study provided care for people in all age groups with physical and/or mental impairments and in some cases with multiple and complex disabilities. The first two aims of the project were to explore the experiences and needs of carers and their encounters with primary health care services, and to elicit their views about how primary health care services could support them and the people they help. The project's third aim was to generate a set of practice guidelines for use by primary health care teams, based on the findings of the first two elements. The study used qualitative methodology – focus groups and in-depth interviews – to explore the experiences and needs of carers from these communities. There were 59 female carers and 27 male carers taking part in the study; 22 female carers and 12 male carers were interviewed in-depth. Some carers participated in both the focus groups and individual interviews; thus in total, 105 carers participated in the project (Table 2.1). We also interviewed 5 females and 3 males who were being cared for. Carers were aged between 20 and over 65. A number were elderly themselves.

The chapter is divided into four sections. We begin with a brief look at the way disability is defined and draw on carers' accounts to explore societal attitudes towards their disabled relatives. This is followed by a discussion of how carers were regarded by society at large and by the communities of which they were a part. In the third section, we explore carers' own attitudes to disability by looking at some of the factors which influenced their perceptions of disability. The final section focuses on the nature of the relationship between carers and their disabled relatives and explores the negotiation of dependency and interdependency in the context of South Asian cultures. Perceptions of disability and care-giving are explored to highlight similarities and differences within and between carers from the four communities. The findings we describe here, however, are based on the experiences of carers and not directly on those of the persons being cared for. It is important to highlight this distinction because carers and those they care for may have differing views about care-giving and receiving. We have used various abbreviations in this chapter (and in Chapter 8) to describe characteristics of carers.[1]

Attitudes to disability

The way that disability is defined and the values attached to it remain highly controversial (Oliver 1990; Morris 1993; Stuart 1996). The medical model of disability has dominated the perception and treatment of disabled people. This model has been criticized for its narrow focus on the medical condition or impairment and for reducing disability to a form of 'personal tragedy' (Oliver 1993). The approach does not acknowledge that people with impairments live in a world with inherent social, physical and psychological barriers which prevent people with impairments from participating in and making a full contribution to society (Swain *et al.* 1993).

Explanations for the persistence of negative perceptions of disability are located in the social construction of 'normality' and 'abnormality'. Any deviation from popular notions of 'norms' in behaviour, mental attributes or physical appearance becomes associated with stigma or ridicule (Goffman 1963). Those with physical or mental impairment are seen predominantly in terms of their 'abnormality' and dependency in most cultures and societies. However, feelings towards disabled people are not always well defined and depend on the type and extent of impairment or condition. For example, mental impairments are generally seen as more stigmatizing than physical impairments. The apparent ambiguity in attitudes arises from the fear of the unknown or 'not normal', on the one hand, and a genuine concern about the welfare of the disabled person, on the other (Lonsdale 1990). The discriminatory treatment of disabled people is shared across most cultures (Webb-Johnson 1991: 36).

In this study it was difficult to separate out attitudes towards disabled people and those towards their carers since a majority of carers were describing situations in which their lives were closely intertwined with those of their disabled relatives. Consequently, comments about disabled people were often directed at carers and in many cases they were the main recipients of negative reactions and comments.

Our study suggested that the combination of fear, stigma and a lack of understanding about the cause of impairment were often associated with negative perceptions. Negative attitudes towards disability were expressed by people who were known to carers and who were often from their own community, irrespective of whether they were relatives or not. However, reactions of close relatives were often singled out as being particularly in-sensitive and therefore causing a great deal of pain. In many cases the negative attitudes of relatives appeared to be intimately tied up with the fear of being associated with the source of the impairment, particularly if it was believed to be inherited. For example, Pakistani Muslim and Gujarati Hindu female carers spoke about the reactions of their relatives towards their disabled children and that they were made to feel responsible for producing disabled children (see Chapter 3 for discussion of attribution of impairment). One Gujarati Hindu female carer reported that her sister-in-law (husband's sister) kept reminding her that disability was widespread in her, the carer's, *khootum* (kinship network united by a common blood-line), that her two daughters were affected because it was something she had passed on from her side of the family, and that disability 'did not exist' on the husband's side of the family.

Although not all cases of childhood disability were congenital, the fear of being associated with the stigma further reinforced and perpetuated negative attitudes towards disability. This was evident from the concern expressed by many parental carers that negative attitudes had far-reaching repercussions on the future prospects of their other children. Although the pattern of marriages in the South Asian community is in transition, arranged marriages are still the norm (Westwood and Bhachu 1988). Many parental carers were aware that comments such as 'they [blood-relatives] all have children like that in her *khootum* . . . if they have children they are all going to be like that' would make it difficult to arrange the marriages of their other, non-disabled, children (GHF – ID).

In some cases, the fear of possible repercussions was so strong that many carers were discouraged from disclosing the full extent of the person's impairment. Gujarati Hindu and Pakistani Muslim female carers spoke about how relatives had insisted that the condition of the disabled person was not disclosed: 'my father-in-law stops me telling because I have two daughters as well and the illness which my son has [is inherited] from my side of the family' (PAKMF caring for son with muscular dystrophy – FG).

Conditions with overt physical symptoms were often difficult to hide. However, carers took extra precautions to hide any conditions associated with mental health. Hussain's (1997) study of Asian carers caring for rela-tives with mental health problems reports similar findings. The increased secretiveness, unfortunately, only aroused more suspicion and perpetuated prejudice and myths about mental illness.

As well as locating the cause of their children's disability in their negli-gent behaviour and in their congenital inadequacy, many carers reported that relatives and friends also implied that their children's disability was a manifestation of their (carers') misdeeds: 'Some people think, she must have done some really bad things. That's why those bad deeds have come up in front of her now in the shape of a disabled child' (PAKMF – caring for adult daughter with severe physical disabilities – FG).

Begum (1992), Lamb and Layzell (1995) and Hussain (1997) report how some carers find the attitudes of people towards disabled people and the discrimination that accompanies them, more difficult to deal with than caring for the disabled person *per se*. A common experience recounted by many carers in the four communities was that they found the exaggerated reactions to their child's physical appearance or behaviour, such as staring, ignoring the disabled relative as if she or he did not exist, and confusion from others who simply did not know how best to help, most upsetting: 'They [friends and relatives] ask about the other kids but they don't ask about the one who's disabled, they don't ask, "How is he, how's he getting on?" . . . Don't they see my other son? Isn't he a human being as well?' (PAKMM caring for son with cerebral palsy – FG).

Similarly, a Gujarati Hindu carer was upset by the fact that her relatives often invited her 'healthy' son over to stay with them during vacations but a similar invitation was never extended to her two adult daughters who had learning disabilities.

Another carer mentioned how someone had said to her 'if he was my child, I would kill him', when she took her son on holiday abroad (PAKMF – FG). However, as Lamb and Layzell (1995) have shown, people who believe that disabled people should never have been born are not confined to minority ethnic communities. Their study, in which 98 per cent of the sample were white, revealed very similar views.

Carers' attitudes towards disability

Other people's attitudes towards disabled people can have serious implications for carers in the way they negotiate care-giving. In the process of socialization most people imbibe the dominant cultural and social values, including attitudes towards disability. In many respects then the carers' views of disablement were a reflection of the prevailing views of the society (both negative and positive) in which they were socialized. However, the impact of negative views seemed to be greatest for parental carers. Evidence from other literature on parental carers' attitudes to disability suggests that not only do parents exhibit a range of emotions from total despair and despondency to optimism and hopefulness but also their feelings and attitudes change with time (Shepperdson 1988; Beresford 1994a).

In our study, carers' perceptions of disability ranged from total pessimism, to acceptance and celebration of life in spite of the disability. Many carers accepted the birth of the disabled child as a 'gift' from God and others accepted impairment as a reflection of imperfections within society as a whole. As noted above, some related impairments to misdeeds in current or past life (or lives). Others offered different explanations. For example, a Gujarati female carer, who had converted to a Christian minority sect, explained: 'I don't think that it is anything to do with our past life. God is kind and loving and it is written in our fate. This is just one of those things which happens.'

Since many carers had been caring for a very long period of time, their accounts reflected their current attitudes and not how they felt when they first learnt about their relative's condition. Negative constructions of disability were most apparent in the carers' attitudes to those who were born with the disabling condition(s) and those who had become disabled early in life. This was particularly the case with parental carers who felt that their children's disability was a burden both for them and their disabled children. For example, one Gujarati Hindu female was very distressed because she had two daughters with learning disabilities. She talked about her own experiences and said she hoped no one else would have to 'suffer' the way in which she had. She also felt that had she known her daughters were 'affected' then she would have had an abortion. She explained: 'I know it's a sin in our community and our culture to have an abortion but that one sin only I would have had to suffer, at least it would have saved two lives, two others . . . I mean today what sort of life have they got now?' (GHF caring for two daughters with learning disabilities – ID).

Such views need to be seen in the context of the difficulties that carers and their disabled relatives faced daily in negotiating social, physical and psychological barriers. In voicing such feelings carers were reflecting society's poor estimation of a disabled person's life as a 'life not worth living'. By contrast, disablement in old age was rarely expressed in such negative terms, suggesting that it was viewed as a 'normal' life process: 'As you get older, it's natural that you'll become ill . . . asthma, eye problems you expect in old age. It happens to everyone' (BMM caring for elderly mother – FG).

Carers' accounts highlighted a number of additional factors which affected how they felt about disability. Religious beliefs, gender differences, nature of disability, age of the disabled person and the length of time care had been provided all had some impact.

Gender and disability

Fatimilehin and Nadirshaw (1994) have reported that the gender of a child with learning disabilities is largely immaterial to many Asian parents. However, the accounts of carers in our study suggested that attitudes towards disability were influenced by the socially determined position of men and women and the degree of vulnerability associated with female sexuality, particularly of disabled adult women who were perceived to be less able to protect themselves (see, for instance, Begum 1992). Many carers believed that caring for a sexually mature female was more difficult than caring for a sexually mature male. Much of this centred around concern about their female relatives being 'touched', abused, having their 'reputation ruined' or becoming pregnant. Carers' views were based on their disabled daughters having direct experience of being hit or 'touched' or because they had hearsay knowledge of what could happen. Maintaining their daughter's *izzat* (reputation) was of great concern to them because if they did not maintain it then society would talk not only about their daughter's moral identity but about the carer's too: 'what if somebody catches her and you know does what ever they want to with her while she's having one of those phases [fits], . . . then they'll [society] be talking dirty talk about her as well as me' (GHF caring for adult daughter with mental health problems and epilepsy – ID).

Within the South Asian community, marriage enjoys a high status. The marriage of a daughter has a special significance as it allows parents, to a great extend, to relinquish their social, economic and moral responsibility for her to her husband. It also signifies the daughter making the normative transition to the status of wife and mother. Many parental carers were upset that their daughters would not have an opportunity to get married and therefore would remain the responsibility of their parents. These views were shared by many male and female carers across the four communities, especially by parental carers. For instance, an elderly Pakistani Muslim male carer caring for two adult daughters, both of whom were blind, said: 'You know, if they were OK, at this stage they would have been married off and they wouldn't have been a burden upon us, you know they would have been in their own homes' (FG). Although parents of disabled sons expressed a similar disappointment about their sons' marriage prospects, disabled sons were perceived to be less vulnerable to abuse and therefore less likely to compromise the family's reputation. However, Begum's (1992) findings revealed that disabled adult males did not share the general optimism vested in their masculinity and reported similar levels of insecurity as those expressed by disabled women.

Religion and disability

Religious influence in the construction of disability is evident in all religions including Christianity, Islam and Hinduism (Stubblefield 1977; Lonsdale 1990; Webb-Johnson 1991; Fatimilehin and Nadirshaw 1994). One of the central tenets of Hindu religious philosophy is the idea of the immortal soul and reincarnation – the cycle of birth, death and rebirth through seven life cycles. Where and in what conditions one's soul is reborn depends on the balance of good and bad deeds committed in previous lives. This cycle of reward and punishment for all deeds and thoughts is called *karma* (Schott and Henley 1996). The Sikh religion was established as an offshoot of Hinduism and as a result many Sikhs also share similar beliefs about reincarnation and *karma*.

Webb-Johnson (1991) argues that the belief in *karma* may help to provide an understanding and an explanation for conditions associated with mental health and help the person affected and the family to come to terms with the situation. Fatimilehin and Nadirshaw's (1994) study of Asian parents caring for children with a learning disability also revealed that many parents had relied on the concept of *karma* to find explanations for their children's disability and to seek spiritual and moral support to come to terms with the condition. Atkin and Ahmad (2000) note that Muslim carers often attributed their child's condition to Allah's will.

Many female carers across the four communities drew on their respective religious beliefs to find explanations for their relative's disability and why the responsibility of caring had fallen on them. However, it was interesting to note that with the exception of a few male Pakistani Muslims, male carers rarely mentioned their religion to account for their relative's condition or impairment.

Many Muslim female carers believed that everything, including illness and impairment, was under the control of God. In some carers' judgement, God had absolute authority over everything and even the skills and knowledge of health professionals were powerless to surpass what God had intended: 'Now everything depends on Allah's wish, I don't think doctor can do anything later. If Allah wish then he can give my husband a long life and also doctor can help a bit' (BMF caring for physically disabled husband who is a wheelchair user – FG).

While Muslim female carers accepted disability as 'God's will', Hindu and Sikh female carers' attitudes towards disability were based on the notions of reward and punishment or *karma*. Some carers found it hard to accept the situation and questioned why God had selected them to be the one to care for someone with a disability. Others felt that they and the person being cared for were being punished for some past misdemeanour: 'God still hasn't forgiven me and forgiven him . . . only I know how I have struggled to bring him up. He's 17 now, there's been very little improvement in him' (PSF caring for 17-year-old physically disabled son – FG).

However, not all carers took such pessimistic attitudes. Some carers treated caring as an opportunity to settle *hessab-kitaab* (debit and credit accounts) by balancing 'bad deeds' and 'good deeds'. For example, many Hindu and Sikh carers believed that the disabled person, child or elderly person had come into their lives to enable them to gain credit by providing care in this life and thereby settle debts from a previous life. Others accepted it as a 'gift' or that they had been 'blessed' by God. Some felt that their situation must have been fated and their caring role predetermined: 'Whatever we've been given, we have to accept it as God's gift, you know. I accept it as our *karma*' (GHF caring for adult daughter with a learning disability – FG).

Fatimilehin and Nadirshaw (1994: 212) reported that many Muslim parents in their study gave similar explanations about earning rewards or consolation from God as a recognition of good deeds.

Carers' attitudes to different types of impairments or conditions

The nature of the impairment or condition and the level of perceived stigma attached to it also influenced carers' perceptions of disability. Certain types of conditions such as epilepsy, psychiatric disorders and learning disabilities produced a mixture of responses such as doubts about the accuracy of the diagnosis, doubts about the seriousness of the condition and distancing from more stigmatizing conditions (see also Ahmad *et al.*, Chapter 3). For example, from the accounts of female carers it was evident that the generally lower level of awareness about and greater discrimination against people with mental illness, caused many to make a distinction between 'madness' and 'mental illness' to lessen the impact of the stigma: 'Yes she's very depressed. She's taking psychiatric treatment. She's not mad' (GHF caring for daughter with psychosis – FG).

The length of time that carers had been caring, and the knowledge of the nature of the condition and its long-term prognosis, had a major influence on carers' perceptions of their relatives' disability and how well they adjusted and coped with their situation. It might be expected that carers who had been caring for a very long time had had more time to get used to disability. This was clearly not the case, as many male and female carers lived in the hope that their disabled relative would get better or be cured: 'We still [do] not grasp how or why it happened like that. We're now hanging about in the hope that he will start walking one day' (GHM – ID). This carer was heavily involved in caring for his son, who became 'brain damaged' (*sic*) after the age of 7, and who needed help with all aspects of care. At the time of interview, his son was 22 years of age.

Attitudes towards carers

As the above discussion indicates, carers were aware of what people in their community felt about their disabled relatives and in many cases were made to feel personally responsible for the cause of the condition or impairment. Evidence from other literature on carers suggests that many informal carers, across different cultures and societies, experience a level of prejudice and discrimination similar to that shown to their disabled relatives (Dalley 1988; Morris 1991; Lamb and Layzell 1995). Attitudes towards carers also seemed to be influenced by other factors, such as the gender-based division of labour, notions of duty, obligation, responsibility and normative expectations.

The role of carer, in most cultures, is traditionally ascribed to women because it is assumed that it is an extension of their mothering or nurturing role. However, society accords a rather ambiguous status to carers (Twigg and Atkin 1994). The ambiguity stems from the lack of distinction between 'caring for' and 'caring about' (R. Parker 1981) and is heightened by the inherent contradiction which on the one hand emphasizes carers' moral duty to care but on the other hand does not fully recognize their contribution.

Feminist critics argue that this ambivalence is most striking in perceptions about and treatment of female carers (Finch and Groves 1980; Dalley 1988). They argue that the lack of distinction between 'caring for' and 'caring about' reinforces the assumption that women are biologically and psychologically destined to be carers of children, and sick or disabled people. This is not to suggest that all women perceive care-giving as an oppressive process or provide care against their will. Indeed, evidence suggests that most female carers provide care out of love and genuine affection (Briggs and Oliver 1985; Beresford 1994a, 1994b); this may also reflect the construction of caring as a moral imperative, so closely aligned with female moral identity. Nevertheless, the imposition of an overwhelming sense of moral obligation on carers leaves very little room for them to negotiate this responsibility. This was clearly evident from the experiences recounted by many female carers across the four communities in our study who claimed that they were discouraged from voicing negative feelings, to ensure that the strength of obligation to care was not weakened:

F3:   Of course it is our society who make you feel you have to do this. If we, for example, can't live like the white community.

F1 *and* F3:   Yes, yes . . . if we, that's right. If we behave like the white people we can easily live.

F3:   You have to think of your parents' respect and status in the society because then they [people] will say that so and so's daughter is behaving badly and not looking after the in-laws' family properly.

(GHF carers – FG)

This dialogue demonstrates both the power of normative values in shaping carers' roles and a misunderstanding that white females are not subject to similar normative expectations.

In many countries, including those in the Indian subcontinent, the lack of state-funded social care provision means that responsibility for the care of elderly and disabled people rests on the goodwill of individual families. This has been described as a form of compulsory altruism (Land and Rose 1985). It is evident that emotional blackmail acts as a form of social control for those who are familiar only with the tradition of compulsory altruism, and have a vested interest in ensuring that it is not diluted or lost.

Men's normative primary role is restricted to the procurement of material resources for their families and therefore they are not expected to play a major role in caring for their sick and disabled relatives. Indeed, not only is there a generally lower expectation of men to care but also it has been reported that, unlike female carers, they are more likely to be treated with sympathy and understanding when they do so (Charlesworth *et al.* 1984; Arber *et al.* 1988). Male carers are perceived to be less able to cope with caring tasks and therefore tend to evoke greater sympathy from professionals and are offered more practical support from formal services. It has also been argued that greater allowance is made for men if they abdicate or extricate themselves from sharing the burden of care-giving. For example, Horowitz (1985) reported that in her study of sibling carers, sisters often made greater allowances for their brothers who failed to take their share of responsibility.

However, evidence also suggests that many men, particularly husbands and fathers, do provide care and in some cases they are the sole or primary carers of their disabled relatives (Arber and Gilbert 1989; G. Parker and

Lawton 1992; G. Parker 1993b; Katbamna and Bhakta 1998). Although some male carers may be treated with more consideration or be more likely to receive support from formal and informal sources, the accounts of male carers in our study, who were caring for their disabled wives or children, revealed that these two groups were not extended the same level of sympathy and support and under certain circumstances were treated with derision. Many male spouse carers reported that they were subjected to unkind and disparaging remarks from other men because, in assuming the role of a carer, they had transgressed the masculine code of behaviour. Male carers who had given up paid work to care and were consequently receiving welfare benefits were perceived to be particularly unworthy of sympathy and respect. One Gujarati Hindu male carer talked about how his relatives teased him; talking about himself in the third person he said: 'they feel that . . . the man [has] changed because now he is looking after his wife and [has become] a "woman's man" or he has got lots of money [benefits] now he doesn't want to sit with us'.

Nonetheless, there was differential treatment of male and female carers in our study. Female carers generally evoked less sympathy than male carers; females were not seen to be doing anything unusual or exceptional in providing care for a disabled relative. Further evidence of the difference in attitudes towards male and female carers was in the way blame was apportioned. For example, mothers whose children were born disabled were mostly blamed for their children's condition or impairment (see p. 15). In sharp contrast, very few fathers claimed that they were subjected to similar criticisms or were made to feel responsible for producing a disabled child. Many mothers believed that, although there was no evidence to link their children's condition to them, it was assumed that, since they had given birth to the child, it must be their fault. For some mothers of disabled children, the birth of a disabled child had far-reaching consequences on their marriage; a number claimed that their husbands were being pressurized into remarrying because they were young, able and intelligent and could quite easily find another partner.

Female carers who were single or divorced, or disabled or elderly themselves, were also treated unkindly. One disabled carer had four children and talked about the attitudes that she experienced both as a disabled person and as a carer. She claimed that people in her community were displeased when she got married and spread rumours that her husband had married her on false pretences because his real motive was to gain entry into Britain. When one child from a pair of twins was born severely disabled, people she knew suggested that, because she was disabled herself, she ought to give up the 'affected' twin for adoption. Older and widowed carers were also treated with less respect and those in female-only households claimed that they were expected to modify their behaviour and adopt a position of appeasement to retain their standing in the community.

Carers also sometimes experienced unreasonable and often conflicting expectations. Many felt that they were constantly 'watched' or policed and their every action and behaviour scrutinized and commented upon by people in their community to make sure that they carried out their duties towards their disabled relatives: 'We don't allow them [disabled daughters] to get dirty. We would not like people to say, look they don't look after them properly' (PAKMM caring for two blind daughters – FG).

At the same time, carers also felt that they were offered very little support to enable them to care. Female carers spoke about how relatives did not take the concerns of the disabled person seriously (for instance, concerning ill-health) and were of the attitude that 'she's always like that' (GHF – FG). Another carer spoke about how relatives kept telling her that she was 'too soft' with her 7-year-old autistic son. Chamba *et al.* (1998b) report similar concerns by parents of deaf children; relatives offered little practical help but much moral policing of the parental performance in coping with the deaf child. Recent findings from a major national survey of minority ethnic families with severely disabled children show that South Asian parents received limited family support in caring tasks (Chamba *et al.* 1999).

Carers' ability to cope with their caring role clearly depends on how they and their disabled relatives are perceived by society at large, which in turn determines their access to social support networks. The attitudes that carers encountered often led them to restrict their social life and some would visit only those who 'accepted' the disabled person. More often than not, carers were not in a position to go out and fulfil social obligations and this led to conflict with relatives. Male and female carers from all groups spoke about social obligations, such as visiting relatives or attending weddings, as an added pressure. They experienced hostility and resentment from friends and relatives because they could not fulfil these obligations due to caring responsibilities.

Care-giving relationships

Informal care-giving takes place within an existing relationship based, usually, on love, affection and respect. It is supported and sustained by ties of reciprocal obligations and expectations. However, the strength of the obligations and expectations vary according to the nature of kinship ties. For example, care-giving relationships between husbands and wives are different from those with children or other kin (Lewis and Meredith 1988; G. Parker 1993b; Beresford 1994a; Twigg and Atkin 1994).

The way that carers and disabled people make sense of disability, and its implications for carers, can have a profound impact on their relationship. The existing carers' literature identifies three different models of care-giving relationships ranging through dependence, interdependence and independence (Lewis and Meredith 1988; G. Parker 1993a; 1993b; Beresford 1994b; Twigg and Atkin 1994). The quality and success of care-giving relationships often depend on the extent to which carers and the persons being cared for can negotiate the boundary between dependence and independence. For example, in extreme circumstances the failure on the part of carers to recognize and appreciate the demarcation between independence and dependence can lead to the 'engulfment' syndrome, in which the carer's emotional identification with the cared-for person is so strong that the carer's identity is subsumed into that of the cared-for person (Twigg and Atkin 1994).

In our study, some carers were very protective of their relative, in some cases to such an extent that, even though the individuals requiring care could have managed to do things for themselves, the carers continued to 'take over' or became totally 'engulfed' in the caring role. One carer said: 'I know she can do a lot of things but then again I would never ask [her] to do lots of things; I'd rather do it myself' (PAKMF – ID). Carers experiencing engulfment tended to be those caring for children, and spouse carers, where much of their lives had been devoted to caring. They consequently could not distance themselves from the caring situation without losing much of their *raison d'être* (G. Parker 1993b).

A high degree of engulfment is unhelpful for both the carer and the cared-for person because it encourages or fosters dependency and a sense of obligation on the cared-for person and unnecessarily increases the burden on carers. Further, a care-giving relationship based on dependency can easily turn into an exploitative relationship, on either side. Carers who had problematic relationships reported how the people they were caring for sometimes used manipulative tactics to get what they wanted. Female carers spoke about how the person they cared for would become very disruptive or have tantrums. In order to prevent such occurrences, carers tried to be very careful about how they spoke or behaved: 'If she says that "I want something for £200" then straight away, I have to go and buy it for her. Otherwise, you know, in her anger she will bang her head, or fall off the bed and you know, that sort of thing' (GHF caring for 19-year-old daughter with physical disabilities – FG).

Another carer recounted how, on requesting her elderly father-in-law, who had incontinence problems, to move closer to the toilet in order to prevent him from urinating on the floor he said: 'Just take me back to India, just leave me there' (PSF – FG). Although female carers, particularly wives, mothers and daughters-in-law, appeared to be most vulnerable to exploitation, a small number of male spouse carers from the Gujarati Hindu and Bangladeshi Muslim communities also felt that their disabled spouses used emotional blackmail to justify their dependency on them: 'You don't want to care for me that's why you want someone else [nurse] from outside to do your job' (GHM – FG).

However, not all care-giving experiences were based on relationships in which disabled persons assumed the role of a dependant. Evidence from the carers' literature also provides examples of care-giving relationships which are based on symbiosis, reflecting the interdependency between carers and those they help (see, for instance, Lewis and Meredith 1988; G. Parker 1993b). This type of care-giving relationship was also evident from the accounts of spouse carers, particularly female spouses in our study. Many carers spoke about the love, affection and companionship provided by their disabled spouses. Female spouse carers were also aware that the presence of their disabled husbands, while they were alive, gave them a respectable status and a degree of protection and security within their communities. Although these views were shared by a majority of female spouses across the four communities, those within the Bangladeshi Muslim communities who had recently settled in Britain were particularly aware of their dependency on their disabled husbands: 'If something happened to my husband where shall I go with my two small kids? My son is very young, he can't even go shopping. I don't know how long I will have to wait . . . when he will grow up and help me' (BMF caring for husband with severe diabetes and asthma – FG).

Evidence from Miller (1987) and G. Parker (1993b) suggests that similar sentiments reflecting the interdependency between spouses were also voiced by white female spouse carers who were used to seeing their husband as an authority figure in their marriages. It is also important to stress that few disabled people are in an entirely dependent relationship. In many families the disabled person may be making a significant contribution in providing care for another member of the family (see, for instance, Morris 1989; Walmsley 1993). Carers of elderly and disabled parents also perceived their care-giving relationship as more than just dependency. The need to reciprocate or 'pay back' was, for many carers, an important aspect of this relationship: 'Well everybody in the family looks after their elders it's just a tradition . . . he [father] has looked after us, he's brought us up and it's our responsibility to look after him in his old age. It's part of our culture' (BMM caring for father with kidney failure – ID).

Negotiation of a care-giving relationship which promotes a degree of autonomy for the disabled person and relieves the carer of some of the responsibility of care-giving has the greatest potential for sustaining a harmonious relationship. Beresford (1994a) provides examples of how parental carers managed and negotiated care-giving to promote independence for their disabled children. Similar examples were recounted, mainly by parental carers in our study. One Gujarati Hindu female carer felt that both her daughters with learning disabilities should be integrated within society: 'give them a chance to learn and mix with others . . . if they go out they'll learn to speak to people' (GHF – ID). Similar views were also expressed by a daughter who felt that her elderly father with dementia should be found a place within society. She made sure that he had opportunities to go to the mosque and take part in social activities.

Although many caring relationships described here seem to fit into the models outlined above, not all care-giving relationships can be interpreted and explained using them. In South Asian cultures, notions of dependence and independence may not be interpreted in the same way as they are in western industrialized nations. Kalyanpur (1996: 256) suggests that in cultures which have traditionally emphasized the importance of family and community as opposed to the rights of individuals, the status and needs of disabled and elderly people are perceived to be less of a burden. The tradition of reciprocity and mutual obligations ensures that those in a dependent position are not devalued.

Conclusion

This chapter has shown that carers and disabled people from South Asian communities experience discrimination and negative attitudes in the same way as do carers from other communities. While issues of attribution or causation are sometimes constructed differently in South Asian communities (for example a result of a misdemeanour in a past life), other explanations ('you must have done something wrong during pregnancy', 'it's from your side of the family, not ours', and so on) have also been revealed in studies of parents with disabled children in white communities. Similarly, fear of the disabled person, unwillingness to involve them in family or social events, additional stigma related to mental health problems, and suspicions about carers' motives in relation to disability and carers' social security benefits, are all described in the wider literature about disability and caring. What may be different, however, is the closeness with which others observe and comment upon the disabled person and the carer. Carers' organizations have successfully raised awareness of issues confronting carers in the population at large. Similarly, disabled people's organizations have campaigned vigorously to change the way in which disability is perceived. Our evidence suggests that there is room for much more targeted activity of this sort in minority ethnic communities.

The length of time that carers had been caring, their knowledge of the nature of the condition and its long-term prognosis, had a major influence on carers' perceptions of their relatives' disability and how well they adjusted and coped with their situation. It might be expected that carers who had been caring for a very long time had more time to come to terms with it. This was clearly not the case as many carers lived in the hope that disabled relatives would get better or be cured of their condition or impairment. Some carers found it very difficult to accept the diagnosis, particularly if it was related to mental health problems. This has implications for the way information and support is provided to carers, not only at the time of the initial diagnosis, but also while they continue to care, helping them come to terms with the condition and its likely prognosis and at the same time allowing them to talk about any anxieties or concerns.

Some carers had close and loving relationships with the person they were caring for. The more positive relationships appeared to be among those looking after younger children. However, even among parents, those who had been caring over a longer period of time reported that they felt that caring became too stressful as they aged. Other relationships had always been difficult to manage or had deteriorated due to difficulties in meeting the needs of demanding relatives. It appeared that carers were often continuing to care with very little consideration being given to their own lives. Inevitably, then, a number of female carers reported deep unhappiness and dissatisfaction in their caring role.

The carer's position within the family had an impact on the caring responsibilities. The roles and expectations of relatives of a South Asian daughter-in-law differ from those of a white daughter-in-law and relatives' expectations of female carers were far greater than those of male carers. Female carers thus often had more than one role. It is particularly important to remember that the presence of other family members in a household does not necessarily mean that the task of caring is divided equally. Female carers and lone carers, in particular, may be experiencing greater difficulties and their needs for support need to be recognized both by other relatives and services.

Acknowledgements

This study was supported by the NHS Executive's Initiative on Physical and Complex Disability.

Note

1 BMF   Bangladeshi Muslim female carer
  BMM   Bangladeshi Muslim male carer
  GHF   Gujarati Hindu female carer
  GHM   Gujarati Hindu male carer
  PAKMF   Pakistani Muslim female carer
  PAKMM   Pakistani Muslim male carer
  PSF   Punjabi Sikh female carer
  PSM   Punjabi Sikh male carer

  FG   Focus group
  ID   In-depth interview
  F1, F2, F3 Carer numbers for participants in focus groups

3

'Causing havoc among their children': parental and professional perspectives on consanguinity and childhood disability

Waqar I.U. Ahmad, Karl Atkin and Rampaul Chamba

Chapter 2 explored perceptions of disability and care-giving among South Asian communities. In this chapter, we focus on how parents and service providers make sense of children's disability or chronic illness. We argue that these constructions are located in people's social lives and their relationships with services; often, professionals provide racialized constructions of disability and chronic illness among minority ethnic communities. The communities have to confront these constructions, often against feelings of guilt and anger, to maintain a valued self-image and to ensure the best care for their children.

The tendency to locate health inequalities between groups in cultural or biological difference is not new (Littlewood and Lipsedge 1989; Ahmad 1993). It is particularly popular in 'explaining' health problems of minority ethnic populations. Such reductionist discourses have 'explained' poorer health of the minority ethnic groups ranging from tuberculosis to rickets, and from syphilis to child mortality. In the west, non-white people have often been aligned with depravity, disease and death; saving them from themselves was an important justification for both slavery and imperialism. Medicine was at the service of racism by neutralizing racist beliefs and practices through their incorporation into medical theories and practice. Historical examples of this would include turning resistance to oppression, such as slaves running away from slavers, into mental pathology ('drapetomania'); the systematic destruction of non-biomedical healing systems in Africa and India; and through 'race' science and ideology, legitimization of the worst excesses of imperialism (see Ehrenreich 1978; Doyal and Pennel 1979; Littlewood and Lipsedge 1989; and Ahmad 1993 for discussion). Many of these discourses employ a pseudo-biological notion of culture so that the location of inequalities simultaneously in deviant cultures and deviant genes is not contradictory. The reduction of minority ethnic problems, ranging from education to welfare needs and health in the non-white people's cultural pathology, so popular in the 'multicultural' discourses of the 1970s, was strongly challenged in the anti-racism of the 1980s (see Centre for Contemporary Cultural Studies (CCCS) 1982 for critique).

Just as some areas of health care were becoming aware of the fallacy of locating health needs in presumed cultural deviance, the 1980s and 1990s have seen the emergence and solidification of a new discourse which combines biological and cultural reductionisms into a single focus of fascination and fear: the practice of consanguinity among the Pakistani population. Research attempting to explain the poor observed birth outcome or increased rates of childhood disability predominantly with reference to consanguinity continues (see reviews by Proctor and Smith 1992; Ahmad 1994). Perhaps more importantly, at an informal level within the NHS, there is a broad acceptance of the consanguinity hypothesis. The strength of this belief (although not universally adhered to) is such that action to improve 'their' health is often reduced by many professionals to arguments about changing 'their' marriage habits (discussed later), while some marshal personal anti-racist credentials by agreeing changes in marriage patterns to be the solution, but arguing that advocating such profound cultural change would be racist. For them inaction equates with anti-racism (see discussion by Ahmad and Husband 1993). The attraction of the consanguinity hypothesis is that it allows health care agencies to abdicate responsibility for appropriate care: if 'they' are dangerous to their own health, then they must change to improve their lot. As before, salvation rests in being more 'like us', a popular message in health education aimed at minority ethnic communities (M. Pearson 1986).

This chapter explores some major themes in literature on consanguinity, ethnicity and health care, thus providing the necessary context for understanding parental and professional discourses on consanguinity and childhood disability. The empirical evidence comes from two qualitative studies, one focusing on deafness in pre-school Asian children, the other examining service provision to families of children with thalassaemia major or sickle cell disorders. The three conditions provide particularly pertinent case studies. They are more prevalent in minority ethnic groups; thalassaemia and sickle cell disorders are recessively inherited and the widely believed greater prevalence of deafness among Asian children is thought to have a recessive component; for sections of the Asian communities consanguineous marriage is the main form of family formation.

We focus initially on providing a summary of the debates on consanguinity and health. The literature in this area is considerable and it is beyond the scope of this chapter to review it here. However, the arguments as they relate to this chapter are briefly summarized. A brief note is also provided on deafness and haemoglobin disorders as they relate to the study populations. Following a description of the empirical studies on which this chapter is based, the findings are structured under two main headings. First, we explore parental perspectives on haemoglobin disorders and deafness. Here we consider both their understandings of why their child has the condition and how they responded to the assertion that the condition may be caused by parental consanguinity. Second, we explore the accounts of a variety of professionals, among them purchasers and policy makers in health and other fields, consultants, general practitioners, specialist haemoglobinopathy workers and teachers of deaf children.

Consanguinity and health: a summary

Much of the debate on consanguinity in Britain relates to the Pakistani population. Most research concentrates on pregnancy and birth outcome and has been discussed by Ahmad (1994). Two main points emerge from Ahmad's review.

First, the evidence not only from much of the epidemiological work conducted in Britain, but also from more sophisticated studies with larger samples in Japan and South India, is at best inconclusive and generally contradictory. There are as many studies which suggest a link as those which suggest no link. In British studies, data on consanguinity are often incomplete and of highly variable quality. In one much cited study by Chitty and Winter (1989), 82 per cent of European, 70 per cent of Pakistani and 77 per cent of Indian mothers did not have their consanguineous status recorded. Studies are thus often based on potentially biased samples. Aamra Darr and Modell (1988) found missing data on consanguinity on 59 out of 100 randomly selected records; a further 16 had information wrongly recorded. The study by Proctor and Smith (1997) also confirms these difficulties and inaccuracies in data recording. Even when evidence from well-designed and conducted studies, based on reliable data, is considered, the results are inconclusive. In a review of evidence, Macleur (1980) argues that as many, including large-scale studies, have shown inconsistent results on consanguinity and foetal loss, there would seem to be little point in collecting and analysing more and bigger datasets.

Second, racism in everyday life and service delivery needs recognition as a strong contributory factor to poor birth outcome among the Pakistani population. The inverse care law in health care is well recognized. Many have reported systematic inequalities in health care provision to minority ethnic communities which lead to poor quality services. For example, Asian women are registered later than white women for pregnancy care; they are referred to ante-natal care later; their general practitioners (GPs) are less likely to have higher qualifications or to be on the obstetrics list. Women who start attending ante-natal care late forgo the chance of certain tests. Asian women's knowledge of available tests is also relatively low – one of the many problems of inequitable health care provision. Further, health professionals' stereotypes of Asian women and terminations lead to discretionary withholding of certain tests. Modell and Anionwu (1996) note that during the first trimester, 80 per cent of Pakistani women accept prenatal diagnostic tests for thalassaemia; in the second trimester, 80 per cent refuse. Our own work shows numerous barriers to adequate information for parents and the use of racialized myths on part of professionals as aids to decision making on provision of information and services (Atkin et al. 1998b). Communication in health care settings remains a problem, leading to many being denied information about care choices and decision making. It is highly likely that inequalities in health care provision are responsible for some part of excess morbidity and mortality among Pakistani new-borns.

Part of this wider racialized disadvantage concerns the treatment of patients by professionals. Various studies show that health professionals employ racial stereotypes in their assessment and treatment of minority ethnic patients (for example Wright 1983; Ahmad et al. 1991; Bowler 1993). This is consistent with findings that professionals are influenced by their professional ideologies and personal views; discretionary decisions rest as much on social and moral judgements as on clinical considerations (Macintyre 1977; Lipsky 1980; Ahmad and Husband 1993). Aamra Darr (1990) notes that health professionals' stereotypes of Asian women influence their decisions about offers of ante-natal tests and termination in relation to thalassaemia. However, parental and professional perspectives on consanguinity in relation to childhood disability remain relatively unexplored, an issue we address in this chapter.

Haemoglobin disorders and deafness

Sickle cell disorder and thalassaemia major are recessively inherited disorders of the haemoglobin where if two healthy carriers have children they have a one in four chance of having a child with the condition, one in two of children being carriers, and one in four chance of the child being without the trait or condition. Sickle cell disorders are largely found among African and Caribbean populations in Britain; thalassaemia largely affects Greek Cypriot and increasingly Asian populations. Both these disorders of the haemoglobin (or haemoglobinopathies) can have serious disabling and life-threatening consequences (for detail, see Anionwu 1993; Midence and Elander 1994). Issues in organization of services and parental experiences of living with their child's condition are explored by Atkin and colleagues (Ahmad and Atkin 1996a; Atkin and Ahmad 1998; Atkin et al. 1998a, 1998b; Atkin and Ahmad 2000).

Equally deafness can also have a genetic component, and there is an emerging interest in the genetics of deafness. There is little hard evidence on relative rates of deafness in different ethnic communities although it is estimated that the Asian populations have two to five times the rate in the general population. Debates in relation to minority ethnic deaf children and adults, identity and relationship with the deaf culture are explored in detail by Ahmad et al. (1998) and Chamba et al. (1998a; 1998b).

The studies

The data come from two qualitative studies focusing on parents of pre-school deaf Asian children and children with thalassaemia major or sickle cell disorder and their interaction with professionals. A unique strength of these studies is that parental and professional views were collected in each study thus enabling us to consider issues of culture, consanguinity and health care in the wider context. The fieldwork was conducted in the north of England during 1995–6. In each study we interviewed key stakeholders around the affected child, namely parents, service providers (usually one from the NHS and one from another agency) and other key respondents such as health and social care commissioners. Interviews with parents were conducted in their preferred languages (English, Urdu, Punjabi or Bengali) and, where requested, by same gender interviewer. Interviews with professionals were conducted in English.

More details of methods for the study of parental and professionals perspectives on haemoglobinopathies are given in Chapter 7. Briefly, the parents' sample consisted of 37 parents of thalassaemic children and 25 parents of children with sickle cell disorder. The practitioner samples consisted of 51 respondents. Also interviewed were 26 parents of deaf children (21 mothers and 5 fathers). Of the 44 professionals interviewed, 18 were from the health service (such as ear, nose and throat (ENT) surgeons, paediatricians, audiological technicians, managers and geneticists), 14 from the education service, 6 social services staff and 6 health commissioners. The vast majority of the parents of deaf children were Pakistani as were parents of children with thalassaemia major. The great majority of sickle cell cases occurred among African Caribbean children. All interviews were tape-recorded. Full transcripts were used for analysis.

Consanguinity was not a main focus of this research; it was raised by parents and practitioners in our discussion of a range of other issues. This in itself reflects the significance of consanguinity as an important, albeit problematic, explanatory discourse.

Parents' accounts

Parents' accounts are structured under two broad sections. First, we explore how they explain deafness and haemoglobin disorders. Second, we consider their responses to the assertion that their child's condition is related to parental consanguinity.

Explaining deafness and haemoglobinopathies

We start by considering the understandings of parents of deaf children. These parents reported that they were given a wide range of possible reasons for the child's deafness, such as nerve damage, asphyxiation during birth, hereditary causes and rubella during pregnancy. The parents' views on causation differed widely. Some said that they were never given a full or satisfactory explanation; many had questions about causation, answers to which they felt would help them understand their child's condition better. They gave ideas about how such information could be delivered. The general literature on childhood disability, as well as specific work on haemoglobinopathies, shows similar parental concerns about diagnosis and disclosure. Parents often complain of little information about the child's condition and the manner in which diagnosis is disclosed is criticized by many parents (Quine and Pahl 1995; S.A. Hill 1994; Atkin *et al.* 1998a, 1998b; Chamba *et al.* 1999).

Although there were a variety of views on why their child was deaf, consanguinity featured frequently in many parents' views on causation. This stemmed from information given to parents by practitioners, personal understandings about inheritance and family history of deafness where it existed, or from other sources. Some alluded to or considered consanguinity as the 'cause' of their child's deafness: ''cos me and me husband are first cousins so it might be genetic . . . if I get a reason for it I'm happy 'cos I know that this what's caused the deafness.'

For others, although the significance of a family history of deafness was acknowledged, they did not discount other potential causes. Nor did a history of deafness make the genetic explanation straightforward to understand. Hill notes that parents interpret and utilize the medical discourses on particular conditions in the light of personal biographies and child's experiences (S.A. Hill 1994). For most of our respondents, personal experiences and knowledge of discordant cases cast doubt on the consanguinity hypothesis; yet parents did not have plausible alternative explanations. Some still struggled to make sense of the child's deafness, their experiences adding to their confusion, as in the case of this mother:

> My first son was born and then three daughters, all three deaf. I thought maybe if it's a boy it's healthy because the first is a healthy boy. Sometimes I thought maybe there's some defect because of some injection or there's some internal disease. The first one is fine and two are deaf. Then when the third one came I thought it's nature. If there was some disease then this one would not have been well and he's okay.

Another mother went through a detailed history of deafness in her family; she was married to a cousin. What she found difficult to understand was that she was hearing as were members of her parental family and yet others in the family line, including several children, were deaf. The fact that hearing family members had deaf children and at times deaf relatives had hearing children added to her bewilderment:

> What am I to think? All us brothers and sisters were okay. But our children have turned out deaf. My husband's older brother's wife's brother is deaf and her children are fine. So, is it just nature? I've met

quite a few women at [school for deaf children] who said there was no one in our families, but still our child is deaf.

Ideas about genetic inheritance and marriage with close kin did not feature as the sole explanation but often coexisted with other factors such as illness and medical complications. For example one parent felt that: 'Because he was in intensive care, I personally feel that they have something to do with it, in the sense that the drugs that were administered and the fact that he didn't breathe straight away'.

Consanguinity as an explanation was more frequently offered for thalassaemia major. Two-thirds of the families reported explicitly being told by a health professional that consanguinity was the cause of their child's condition, a particularly unfortunate statistic in that for many families, this was the only aetiological knowledge about the condition they possessed. Further, being told that their child's condition was associated with their consanguineous status did not convey the genetic inheritance of the condition. Parents often thought that the condition began with them, being 'caused' by a cousin marriage. Few offered genetic explanations; where they were offered parents often possessed mechanistic models of inheritance. For example, parents may recount that there was a one in four chance of an affected child if both parents were carriers for thalassaemia. However, many interpreted this in an absolute sense rather than as a statistical risk which applied to each and every pregnancy. This led to some parents believing that if they already had an affected child then the next three would either be trait free or simply carriers for thalassaemia. Such thinking was shared by both the parents who were well educated and articulate speakers of English and those with little formal education or knowledge of the English language. For example, in one of our feedback sessions to a parents' support group, we met a mother of a thalassaemic child from outside our study area. She had found out about our presentation from a relative who was involved in our study, and was a member of the parents' group. We presented our initial findings and noted that many parents found it difficult to understand the nature of inheritance of haemoglobin disorders. This well-educated and articulate mother was surprised and distressed that her assumption that her next three children would not have thalassaemia major was ill founded.

However, such understanding is not peculiar to Asian parents, nor indeed to minority ethnic communities. Rapp (1988) and Parsons and Atkinson (1992), among others, have noted differences in lay and professional discourses and models of genetics, risk and inheritance. However, it appears that Asian populations are less well informed about genetic conditions affecting them than many other communities (Green and France-Dawson 1994; Dyson 1997).

As noted, we also interviewed parents of children with sickle cell disorder; most of these parents were African Caribbean. While inheritance of thalassaemia and SCD is identical, parents of SCD children offered a variety of views on causation from historical ('the sickle cell gene offers protection against malaria', 'it is related to being African') to biomedical (statistical risk of two carriers passing on the genes), although understandings were not equivalent to those of professionals. Consanguinity was never raised as an issue by African Caribbean parents. Green and France-Dawson (1994) have also reported differential understanding of haemoglobinopathies between African Caribbean and Asian parents.

For Asian parents, the assertion that the child's impairment or illness was 'caused' by parental consanguinity resulted in considerable guilt; parents felt responsible for their child's condition. Genetic knowledge was seen as abstract, something they had little or no control over. The association with consanguinity seemed more personal, carrying an implicit sense of blame. Such guilt was not present in accounts of parents of children with SCD. As a consequence of this guilt, many found it difficult to come to terms with the diagnosis. Several remarked that such guilt never really disappeared, as this mother notes:

> But still when you see your child suffer, when your child has a cold and it develops into a chest infection or something like that and then you're to blame if anything goes wrong because you feel responsible for it. So it's just very similar to that. It took me a long time to get to terms with my feelings of guilt. I mean, and when I think about the future and my daughter's understanding of thalassaemia and how she's going to cope with it, I think to myself, how am I going to face the fact that it's something that she's got from us and how is she going to feel about it.

The theme of parental guilt for the child's condition appears in other literature (for example Whitten and Fischoff 1974 in relation to SCD); however, the more pronounced link with personal biography and marriage choice heightened this for our Pakistani respondents.

An acceptance that thalassaemia may be related to cousin marriages was not always equated with the condition having a genetic basis. Like some of the parents of deaf children, a condition being 'caused' by cousin marriages does not necessarily convey the genetic nature of the condition. Five parents, for example, associated thalassaemia with first cousin marriage without relating it to genetics. As already briefly noted, reasons for this are perfectly understandable; parents thought that the condition started with them without recognizing the inherited nature of their own carrier status. Similarities with models of inheritance among the white population are striking (Green 1992). Similarly, Davison (1997) notes that many of his respondents articulated links between a condition and family history – that a condition runs in a particular family – without linking it to any explicit model of genetic inheritance.

The tendency among many parents not to relate family basis of thalassaemia with genetic inheritance, as noted, is unsurprising. However, it does represent failure on the part of many professionals who may be beating the wrong drum by emphasizing consanguinity as the 'cause' of thalassaemia rather than providing more neutral and accessible information about inheritance and risk.

Responses to assertions that parental consanguinity 'caused' their child's condition

In the case of both deafness and thalassaemia major, parents had differed in their responses to the assertion that consanguinity 'caused' the condition. Among most parents of deaf children, there was a general distrust of genetic explanations and particularly of genetic counselling. For example, one parent of a deaf child supported his distrust of genetic explanations with reference to the situation of a friend who was told that there was a strong chance of her future children being deaf; they had two more children, both were hearing. In some cases, even when there was some ambivalent acceptance that consanguinity may be the likely cause, there was resentment about the way this was emphasized by professionals. One mother comments:

> I mean, I know that it's likely, more than likely, that it's because my husband and I are first cousins and I mean we get [this] thrown in our face every time. I mean we can't blame our parents now for this decision to marry [us] . . . the fact is that we have two lovely boys but every time we go and see with [deaf child], his consultant is [name], and every time I've gone to see him . . . this is the most subject he does bring up . . . At first I thought it was a prejudice towards it but knowing some facts myself and then also knowing that it's not really been scientifically proven, I really don't know what to think.

As noted by S.A. Hill (1994) and others (for example Atkin *et al.* 1998b), such re-examination of medical knowledge in light of personal experience is the norm for many parents. Indeed a rejection or subversion of medical knowledge, and an attempt to emphasize the normality of the affected child rather than their difference, constitutes an important coping mechanism against what many parents regarded as excessively negative prognosis of thalassaemia, as is discussed in Chapter 7 (see S.A. Hill 1994; Ahmad and Atkin 1996a; see Chapter 4 for young people's accounts of living with sickle cell disorder).

Equally, the responses of parents of thalassaemic children were mixed. These ranged from resentment and distrust of health professionals, which compromised future relationships with some professionals, to an acceptance of the asserted link but a recognition that consanguineous marriage represented a cherished tradition with considerable benefits and, for some, acceptance of the consanguinity hypothesis and a desire to change patterns of family formation.

Five parents felt that they had been given misleading information by health professionals. All these parents were angry on discovering that thalassaemia occurred among children of couples who were not related, something which clearly was contrary to what they had been led to believe. The anger focused around the unnecessary guilt and self-blame they had felt about the asserted link between consanguinity and thalassaemia, often projected to fear of being accused of causing the condition by affected children. One mother, despite being complimentary about the information she received when her child was diagnosed as having thalassaemia major, was annoyed that she was made to feel guilty and responsible for the condition. In the quotation below, she conveys a newly found and empowering knowledge of inheritance of thalassaemia:

> I think the approach needs to be very positive and the people in the medical profession need to be more positive in the way that they actually give information to their patients rather than saying that it's happening because you're having cousin marriages. *I don't think it's anything to do with cousins, it's to do with whether the person you're going to marry is a carrier or not* [our emphasis].

Similarly, another mother expressed her anger about the emphasis on consanguinity. For her, as for many other parents, the discovery that non-consanguineous parents can also have thalassaemic children brought considerable relief from previously felt disempowering guilt. However, she, like some other parents, felt that she could no longer fully trust health professionals; these parents had a clear view that information provided was not value free or non-judgemental, some seeing it as racially oppressive. This level of distrust created tensions in their relationships with some professionals (mainly consultants and general practitioners), although views about haemoglobinopathy workers were generally positive (see Atkin *et al.* 1998a, 1998b). Such distrust was also present among parents of deaf children, and for different reasons (mainly racial stereotyping on the part of professionals and poor quality of service) among parents of children with sickle cell disorder.

Several parents of thalassaemic children, however, accepted the consanguinity link uncritically (as did some parents of deaf children). Ten parents, for example, felt that the supposed link between consanguinity and thalassaemia would encourage changing marriage patterns. Several felt that marriages between cousins should stop. Others advocated testing prospective partners of their children, as one mother of a thalassaemic daughter commented: 'I would check her future husband before my daughter got married. I would check his blood test. That's what I would do, I don't mind if he doesn't bother, but I will say it.'

Testing for carrier status prior to marriage is the norm in 'British' Cyprus. However, this is generally not done to avoid marriage with a carrier or between carriers. Knowing their carrier status allows couples to make informed decisions on the basis of prenatal tests. Among our respondents, those who emphasized not marrying cousins seemed to do so without a solid understanding of the nature of inheritance or choices available to carrier couples. The limited and partial understanding of inheritance offered limited choices for preventive action to these families; choices which are consistent with their understanding but which are substantially more limiting and self-blaming than those available to families with a more rounded understanding of the nature of haemoglobinopathies. (For a discussion of ethics of haemoglobinopathy provision, see Atkin and Ahmad 1998.)

The acceptance of the consanguinity hypothesis also shows an uncritical acceptance of medical advice on part of some parents. Watson (1984) reports greater trust of medical professionals among Bangladeshi mothers, compared to white mothers; equally, Baker *et al.* (1984) and Bhopal (1986) have explained the higher rates of immunizations among Asian children with reference to uncritical acceptance of medical information. Such acceptance may be a feature of poor socio-economic position and education, applying mainly to those who rely on professionals for much of their information with little recourse to other sources of knowledge or competing discourses, and where there is a clearer status hierarchy between users and professionals. For example, the research on doctor–patient relationships shows that middle-class patients receive better quality of care and yet are more critical of services (Pendleton and Hasler 1992; see also Ahmad *et al.* 1998 in relation to families of Asian deaf people).

Others accepted the asserted association between consanguinity and thalassaemia but felt that little could be done about it. Marriage with relatives was 'their way of life', and it had other benefits. Marriage could not simply be contracted or refused on the basis of someone's carrier status. One parent, for example, said that such knowledge would not have made her change her choice of marriage partner:

> Well, my GP said that I ought to have my husband tested and everything, but you see, we were engaged before I found out about myself and then we considered getting my husband tested before we got married, you know and to avoid the situation but then we just let it go because I mean there's more to a marriage than just [whether someone is a carrier].

Respondents rarely, if ever, blamed their own parents for their marriage, accepting that parents acted in their children's best interests. However, a few felt that, knowing what they knew now, they would have changed their choice of marriage partner. In contrast to the work of Davison (1997) and Katbamna *et al.* (see Chapter 2), there was no attempt to blame the partner for the child's condition. Because of the shared kin networks of the two partners, blaming the partner was rarely a logical option for the child's condition.

Professionals' views

The fact that professionals' views matter in construction of needs, ideas of deservingness and delivery of services is well established (Lipsky 1980;

Ahmad and Husband 1993). Equally established is the fact that professional practice reflects the dominant racial and gender stereotypes; indeed professional ideology neutralizes and legitimizes such prejudices by giving them respectability as scientific facts (Ehrenreich 1978; Scully and Bart 1978; Littlewood and Lipsedge 1989; Ahmad 1993). A number of themes are important to summarize in order to provide the context for understanding professional views. First, both historical analysis and contemporary work on the relationship between the west and the 'orient' notes the construction of the 'oriental' identity as opposite of the western identity. Themes such as alienness, sexual impropriety, cultural pathology, dysfunctional and oppressive families, especially in relation to status of women, have been recounted by Said (1978), Leila Ahmed (1992) and others. Second, professionals act, at least in part, as agents of the state, and the exercise of their formal power is related to their ideas about deservingness of the user for state provided privileges (Ahmad and Husband 1993). Professional concerns about responsible citizenship, doing the 'right thing' as parents, and following medical advice are often articulated as if they are value free; the historicity, cultural specificity and ideological biases are rarely acknowledged (Crawford 1977; Scully and Bart 1978; Ahmad 1993; Atkin and Ahmad 1998; Atkin *et al.* 1998b). Further, as is well recognized, contemporary forms of racism rely on the language of culture, lineage and belonging; emphasizing the alienness of certain practices or locating observed problems in such alienness are thus important forms of racialized discourse. Apparently clinical and value free concerns about consanguinity expressed by professionals below, therefore, need to be set within this broader context.

Like parents, professionals were heterogeneous in their views. Not all held the same belief in the consanguineous link to thalassaemia major or deafness; however, the more high status professionals, such as consultants and GPs, were often more assertive in proposing such a link. In case of deafness, for example, teachers of deaf children were suspicious of a single cause approach to deafness; consultants (with some exceptions) were largely convinced of the link between consanguinity and deafness. The following ENT surgeon's views combine a myriad of fears about consanguinity and related factors such as status of women, responsible behaviour and doing what the British do:

Yes, without any doubt. I think it's a . . . I mean, I always thought it was a religious requirement that you marry your cousin but I'm told it isn't. I had misunderstood that myself. It's just basically a tradition, isn't it? And that to me seems that if they're going to live in westernized society and derive the benefits of it I think that's something that needs thinking about because more and more, now that there are Asian people working here, particularly Asian girls, they will tell you quite bluntly, quite bluntly, that the last thing they want is an arranged marriage. And it's that one factor which is causing this awful dilemma of deafness. Whether it's responsible for some of the other factors that we have, mainly multiple congenital abnormalities we see in this group of children I can't comment on that. I don't know. But it seems to me a dire tragedy that this isn't being rectified. I had a very good colleague in one of the cities, who was an Indian colleague who actually went out to [the locality] to talk to the Asian families about this one problem, to try to explain to them how detrimental it was . . . It's a . . . well it's not for me to discuss your culture I mean, that's your culture and that's it. I think that it's a shame when a culture can't see that something they're doing which is near and dear to their wishes is causing such havoc among their children. I would have thought the more sensible and far-seeing members of that culture would say, 'Shouldn't we be having another look at this?' It's a terrible tragedy to inflict all those problems on a beautiful new-born child because that poor kid didn't have any say in the matter did he?

This long quotation, typical of the sentiments of several other medial practitioners, sums up the many and varied fears: unacceptability of arranged marriages; arranged marriages not being acceptable in the British context; arranged marriages being responsible for deafness, and possibly for other 'congenital abnormalities'; responsible behaviour being not to have consanguineous marriages; Asian cultures being pathological, 'causing havoc'; an assumption that cultures are homogenous and predictive of behaviour (can 'see' things); unfairness of consanguineous marriage for inflicting disability on children. Such views are difficult to disguise as unbiased professional opinion. Brah (1992) and Ahmad (1993) have noted the white professionals' passion for saving Asian women from their presumed uniquely oppressive cultures. As noted, however, not all professionals shared such views but many of the consultants were vociferous in their condemnation of consanguineous marriage for 'causing' deafness in Asian children. Differences in the consultants' and teachers' perspectives may also reflect those between medical and social models of disability, although within the deaf culture the role of teachers of the deaf is not always regarded as progressive.

In thalassaemia major, the division in views was clear cut with haemoglobinopathy counsellors having a different approach from that of many GPs and consultants. Haemoglobinopathy counselling, in keeping with genetic counselling more generally, has emerged in the shadow of fears about the eugenic connotations of new genetics (Atkin and Ahmad 1998). Although there are unresolvable debates about the possibility of non-judgemental genetic counselling, a philosophy of non-judgemental counselling emphasizing informed decision making on part of parents is expected to underpin the practice of counsellors. This philosophy is not always shared by other clinical professionals, few of whom have formal training in haemoglobinopathy counselling. Information on genetic conditions is provided by a variety of health professionals, few of whom would have detailed knowledge of social and political debates around new genetics and informed decision making. And many have insufficient training in genetics to provide an acceptable standard of service to carriers, parents or affected individuals. All the haemoglobinopathy counsellors were themselves from minority ethnic groups; the majority of Asian parents were served by Asian counsellors. At a broader level, the shortage of counsellors with skills in South Asian languages is a recognized problem (Anionwu 1996a). A shared minority status and cultural background may also have contributed to the more sympathetic attitude of counsellors. However, a shared cultural or religious background in itself is not a sufficient condition for an empathetic relationship between professionals and users (see Ahmad *et al.* 1991).

The haemoglobinopathy counsellors raised concerns about the consultants telling parents that cousin marriages *caused* thalassaemia. Interviews with several consultants and general practitioners confirmed the haemoglobinopathy counsellors' accounts. One consultant, for example, reflected on this:

> The majority of them are of Mirpuri Pakistani origin and of those the great majority of those are consanguineous. So they're quite a high-risk population despite their small size, that's why we get so many children with thalassaemia. We try to talk them out of it [cousin marriages] but they won't listen.

Another consultant remarked:

> It's us going to them wanting, trying to beat the drum going: 'You know that this condition, it's pretty bloody awful, you might want to know about it and think about the implications for your family'. And obviously it comes, it brings this back to the question of consanguinity, 'Do you really want to marry your first cousin?' Couldn't a second cousin do, it drops the risk substantially, third cousin and you're getting back to, what, population risk.

Apart from obvious misplaced emphasis on consanguinity rather than informed choice on the part of parents being the approach to sound genetic service provision, this consultant actually shows little understanding of the nature of consanguinity within the Pakistani population. A consideration about carrier status is unlikely to become the predominant feature in selecting marriage partners.

Some general practitioners shared these concerns about consanguineous marriages. For example, one GP advised his patients against cousin marriages but acknowledged that few took up his advice: 'No, I think it is just simply, so much their custom I suppose and they go along that, you know, so and so's married their cousins for years and years'.

Haemoglobinopathy counsellors challenged these assertions and were especially concerned about the guilt felt by parents, an issue discussed earlier in relation to parental accounts. This also created tensions in the relationship between parents and some health professionals. One counsellor commented: 'It's just the way in some areas where it creates, I suspect a lot of misguided guilt and distrust because people were blamed, I think probably unnecessarily, and inappropriately.'

In one area, a previous research study had explored the potential contribution of consanguinity to differentials in birth outcome, including overt congenital malformations, between Pakistani and white groups. The results showed Pakistani babies to have poor birth outcome compared to white babies; however, there were no differences between the Pakistani parents in a consanguineous marriage and those married to partners who were not related by blood. As a consequence, a certain degree of rethinking on consanguinity had taken place among some professionals in this locality. A community nurse manager acknowledged that the trust's previous preoccupation with first cousin marriages was probably misplaced:

> And there are lots of issues around that whole area of consanguinity and wherever and it's difficult isn't it because it's seen as a European backlash against their culture and community. If you talk about it they say 'well it's a political issue'. It's interesting, we've had [a researcher] doing research on consanguinity and handicapping conditions and in fact consanguinity wasn't the main, the main correlation was poverty . . . so that sort of made some of us pause and think, 'God, better rethink some of this', you know.

The change in this area, however, was not uniform across different professionals. Some of the senior professionals we interviewed were vociferous in their condemnation of consanguinity.

In summary, professional views highlight the following. Although views were not homogenous, there appeared a divide between the medically qualified and senior practitioners on the one hand and haemoglobinopathy counsellors and teachers of the deaf on the other. (Incidentally, some teachers of the deaf, while suspicious of the emphasis on consanguinity, maintained reductionist views about language choice and language support for Asian deaf children where the acquisition of an ethnic identity and parental language was regarded as far less important than British Sign Language skills and membership of the deaf community – see Chamba *et al.* 1998b.) The former were more vociferous in their condemnation of consanguinity. As we have noted, this condemnation was packaged in generalized opposition to arranged marriages, Asians not behaving responsibly as 'British' people, Asian cultures 'causing havoc' in terms of illness and disability, and concerns about the status of Asian women (see Brah 1992). Haemoglobinopathy counsellors and teachers of the deaf were open to alternative explanations. Counsellors, in particular, regretted the approach taken by medical colleagues, which they felt caused guilt and led to resentment among parents. The difference is likely to partly be a reflection of competing philosophies and professional ideals of medically qualified practitioners, and counsellors and teachers of the deaf. Partly, the more sympathetic approach of the haemoglobinopathy counsellors may reflect these practitioners' own ethnic identity; they were Asian or African Caribbean women and were concerned with the often negative and racially marginalizing atmosphere in the NHS. Purchasers had little to say on these matters and were rarely aware of the power dynamics and competing professional discourses within services for deaf children or haemoglobinopathies.

Conclusion

This chapter explored some themes in the literature on consanguinity, ethnicity and health care, before presenting two empirical case studies exploring parental and professional discourses on the origins of thalassaemia major and deafness. This theoretical and empirical exposition illustrates the tendencies of health professionals to explain inequalities between different ethnic groups in terms of biological and cultural differences. Such a reductionist view disadvantages the parents during the diagnosis process, denying them basic information about their child's condition as well as raising the possibility of guilt, that makes it more difficult for the parent to come to terms with the condition. Our study focused on both mothers and fathers. No systematic differences were observed between mothers' and fathers' perspectives, or in how professionals responded to them in relation to consanguinity. Elsewhere, we have reported that mothers often complained of not being taken seriously by professionals (Atkin and Ahmad 2000); however, this related largely to diagnosis of sickle cell disorder and rarely related to assumptions about consanguinity.

Consanguineous marriage may carry some raised risk of congenital conditions. However, this holds true largely if the particular recessive genes are not widely spread in the wider population. If the latter is the case, as for example for beta thalassaemia in the Pakistani population, then marriages with non-kin will provide very limited, if any, genetic advantages (Professor Bob Mueller, University of Leeds, personal communication, 1997). However, our analysis shows that the effort expended in alerting the communities about the asserted dangers of consanguineous marriage may be out of proportion to the added risks involved. Parents are denied access to balanced information on the nature of these conditions and patterns of inheritance, information which would enable them to provide more appropriate care for their children. The inappropriate emphasis on consanguinity leads to resentment on part of parents and a distrust of service professionals. Further, the finding that parents may well have internalized the given explanation that their child's condition is due to parental consanguinity, but still not understand that inheritance is genetically based, shows the futility of professional fascination with consanguinity.

The emphasis on first cousin marriages caused guilt among many of the South Asian parents, who felt personally responsible for their child's condition. By comparison, this sense of guilt was largely absent from the accounts of African Caribbean families with children with SCD; these parents made no reference to patterns of family formation in explaining the child's condition and a discussion of consanguinity was simply not felt to be relevant either by parents or by professionals. Yet the patterns of inheritance for thalassaemia and SCD are identical. The feelings of guilt expressed by Asian parents have relevance in discussing their ability to come to terms with the condition. It was noticeable that the guilt felt by Asian parents made it more difficult for them to come to terms with their child's condition and affected their ability to cope (Atkin and Ahmad 2000). Asian parents' knowledge of thalassaemia remained poor and they often lacked the most basic information about the nature and consequences of the condition, factors which have a strong bearing on parents' ability to look after their affected children. Health professionals often blamed communication difficulties for parents' lack of understanding of the condition. Perversely, such communication difficulties did not prevent most parents of a child with thalassaemia associating the condition with first cousin marriages; this was often their only 'factual' information about the condition, and an association that they found disempowering.

More generally, the emphasis on consanguinity in explaining the origins of thalassaemia or deafness denies South Asian families equal access and care entitlements. Specifically, it denies parents information and knowledge about reproductive decisions and their child's disability. The concerns about consanguinity further racialize, that is reduce to perceived racial or cultural difference, the experience of South Asian families. There is a strong need for health professionals to adopt a more balanced approach to explaining disability among Asian families and offer the range of information to which all parents have a right, information which is empowering and allows the opportunity for informed decision making and facilitates coping with the condition for the affected individual and their family. And information which facilitates decisions about life and strategies to maximize self-determination on part of disabled young people. Disabled minority ethnic people and their families confront even greater hurdles than their white counterparts (see Chamba et al. 1999). Professionals are too often part of the problem for disabled people and their families, to be survived, coped with or side-stepped. Yet the potential for professionals to become allies and facilitators is considerable. Regrettably it remains to be realized. And without challenging both disablism and racism within service delivery and more broadly in society, it is likely to remain unrealized.

Acknowledgements

Our thanks to the Department of Health, which supported the work on deafness through an Ethic Minority Health Access Grant, and the NHS Executive's Initiative on Physical and Complex Disability (PCD/A4/16), which supported research on services to families of children with sickle cell disorder or thalassaemia.

4

Living with sickle cell disorder: how young people negotiate their care and treatment

Karl Atkin and Waqar I.U. Ahmad

Impairments and chronic illnesses vary in their stability and need to be managed. Some, such as sickle cell disorders, require management at two levels. First, in the steady state of illness, the affected individual is encouraged to undertake lifestyle precautions as well as medication to avoid complications. Second, the painful crisis requires active management through administration of powerful analgesics. In this chapter we are not directly concerned with the disabling consequences of SCD. Instead, we focus on how young affected people cope both with the daily demands of living with SCD and with the painful crisis.

Compliance with treatment is a major problem in many childhood chronic illnesses (Geiss *et al.* 1992) and has particular consequences for those with a sickle cell disorder. Affected young people are expected to take daily medication, such as folic acid and penicillin, as well as follow various precautions to reduce the risk of a painful crisis. The onset of pain requires further medical treatment, such as the administration of analgesics. Compliance with daily medication and precautions, however, is poor (Ahmad and Atkin 1996b), while little is known about how young people manage their pain (Midence 1994). In discussing this further, we shall deal with two themes.

First, we explore how young people respond to treatment and precautions. We examine the personal and social contexts within which treatment and precautions assume meaning and significance, and in doing so consider reasons for non-compliance. This approach gives primacy to the young person's experience of the condition within the broader context of social relations and 'growing-up'. We argue that compliance is not simply a technical or practical task but is bound up with the imagery, symbolism and connotations associated with the illness (Bury 1991) and the potential impact of the condition on social roles (Morris 1991). Second, this broad approach is applied to the young person's specific experience of pain. The sufferer often regards the painful crisis as the defining feature of SCD, symbolic of the illness and its consequences (Midence and Elander 1994). Medication becomes caught up in this as the young person attempts to gain relief from the most stressful and potentially life threatening complication of their illness (Maxwell and Streetly 1998). As a starting point, however, a brief description of SCD is necessary.

Sickle cell disorders include sickle cell anaemia, haemoglobin sickle cell disease and sickle beta thalassaemia. All are recessive blood disorders where individuals who inherit a deleterious gene from both parents develop the disease. In the UK the groups most at risk of SCDs are of African Caribbean or West African origin. There are estimated to be between 8000 and 10,000 people with SCD. There are, of course, many more healthy carriers of the condition. SCDs are variable, unpredictable and, at times, life threatening. Primarily, those with SCDs are prone to 'sickling' of the red blood cells. This causes blockages in smaller blood vessels and results in the 'painful crisis', as well as anaemia, leg ulcers, stroke and damage to various parts of the body including the spleen, kidneys, hips, eyes and lungs. Affected children are vulnerable to strokes and life-threatening infections such as pneumonia and meningitis. Treatment and care include the prevention of life-threatening infections, pain management and the avoidance of circumstances that cause the red blood cells to 'sickle'.

Consequently, young people face a range of treatments and precautions. They are encouraged to take folic acid daily, to aid maturation of red blood cells. To prevent infections, daily dosages of penicillin are prescribed. There is no guarantee, however, that such medication will prevent the complications associated with the illness. The aim is to improve the child's general well-being and reduce the risk of complications, including the painful crisis. Severely affected young people may also take hydroxyurea to increase the foetal haemoglobin level and reduce the risk of sickling. Pain relief is given when required, in both the home and the hospital. Besides treatment regimens, young people are encouraged to take various precautions to avoid the painful crisis. These include keeping warm, drinking plenty of fluid, as well as more general precautions – often based on personal experience – such as not exerting oneself and knowing one's own limits.

Sickle cell disorders: strategies for avoiding complications

Perhaps not surprisingly, regular use of medicine and the need to follow precautions are seen as restrictive, imposing limitations on daily living activities (Ahmad and Atkin 1996b). Treatment regimens thus become an important aspect of the young people's illness narrative and are part of how they understand, experience and cope with their chronic illness (Strunk et al. 1985). Medical regimens and general precautions need to be seen as part of the wider process by which young people make sense of the relationship between their body, self and illness as they struggle to lead valued lives and maintain and construct a positive self-image (Bury 1991; Locker

1997). As part of this struggle, however, young people are also dealing with the more general problems associated with growing up (Ebata and Moss 1991). Coping with the new experiences and responsibilities of growing up becomes difficult, as previous certainties are questioned (Dornbusch *et al.* 1991). For example, the emerging emotional difficulties associated with seeking some autonomy, renegotiating relationships with parents, establishing peer relationships, coping with school and making decisions about future ambitions can impinge on the compliance process, as well as the young person's experience of pain (Ahmad and Atkin 1996b).

Introducing debates about the process of growing up offers a more general reminder that a young person's experience of chronic illness does not occur within a social or psychological vacuum (Sloper and Turner 1992). The family is a particularly important feature of the child's illness narrative (Thompson 1994). Not only is the care of a young person negotiated within the context of family obligations and reciprocities (Finch and Mason 1993), but also young people, themselves, do not take decisions about their health independently of their families (Brannen *et al.* 1994). As important mediators between the child and health professionals, parents assume a central role in negotiating compliance with their children (Midence *et al.* 1996). The relationship between child and parent is fundamental to this and compliance can itself become a site around which relationships are developed and challenged (Geiss *et al.* 1992; Ahmad and Atkin 1996b; Atkin and Ahmad in press).

Non-compliance is especially common among adolescents with SCD, as they strive to be 'normal', adopt lifestyles which are consistent with their own wishes and identities and are valued by their peers, and take greater personal control of their own care (Ahmad and Atkin 1996b). The issue of non-compliance among adolescents is also noted in other childhood chronic illnesses such as cystic fibrosis (Mador and Smith 1989; Geiss *et al.* 1992), asthma (Lemanek 1990) and diabetes (Hoare and Mann 1994). Consequently, parents never fully trust their child to comply with medical regimens (Midence and Elander 1994; Atkin and Ahmad 2000). Young people sometimes feel that their parents become 'over-protective' (Midence *et al.* 1996), a common theme in the literature on childhood chronic illness and disability (Eiser 1990; Davis and Wasserman 1992) and growing up (Brannen *et al.* 1994).

Coping with pain reflects these main themes (Anionwu 1993). The onset of pain requires practical and emotional responses, as young people attempt to make sense of changes in the relationship between body and self, and learn to accept and cope with their condition (Hurtig and White 1986). To this extent, pain makes demands on the child that, in the short term, have to take priority over other aspects of their life (Conyard *et al.* 1980). Pain can also have a symbolic significance (Thompson 1994). Young people have to deal with not only the *consequences* of pain but also the *possibility* of pain. They often worry, for example, about the pain returning even when they are well (Fuggle *et al.* 1996). The family emerges as an important feature of the young person's experience of pain, providing both practical and emotional support (Walco and Dampier 1990). Finally, the treatment of pain implicates the role of health professionals (Ahmad and Atkin 1996b). Controlling pain in a major crisis usually requires hospitalization. However, many young people and their parents are critical of hospital treatment, complaining of delays in and inadequacy of pain relief, severity of pain not being taken seriously, ignorance of professionals and insensitivity of staff (Midence and Elander 1994; Atkin *et al.* 1998a, 1998b). Such responses are argued to be indicative of institutional racism (Anionwu 1993).

The study

The aim of the study was to provide a detailed understanding of young people's experience of living with a genetic condition with potential disabling and life-limiting consequences, within the broader context of growing up. We conducted in-depth interviews with 26 young people with SCD (age range 10 to 19 years). (The study also included 25 young people with thalassaemia major; however, this chapter does not include their experiences.) Each young person was interviewed twice over a six-month period, which enabled the narrative to reflect the variability of the condition and its possible influence on their experience. The sample was drawn from the records of health professionals, such as paediatricians and specialist haemoglobinopathy (disorders of the haemoglobin) workers, in six localities in the Midlands and north of England. In all areas but one, the sample represented all known cases of SCD. In the one remaining area, the respondents were randomly selected in order to reach the target sample. The eventual sample included 14 girls and 12 boys. Of these, 18 had sickle cell anaemia, 5 had sickle beta thalassaemia, 2 had SD Disease and 1 had SE Disease. The average age of the sample was 14.2 years and the mode was 12 years. In terms of ethnicity, 19 of the young people described themselves as 'African Caribbean', 6 described their ethnic origin as 'mixed' and 1 said she was an 'Indian Hindu'. Of the 26 young people, 19 were still at school, 5 were at college and 2 were seeking work. Young people were offered an interviewer of their own sex. All interviews were in English and were tape-recorded.

The project used qualitative methods and analysis, based on semi-structured interviews; such methods allow an examination of complex and contingent situations, behaviours and interactions (Mishler 1986). A topic guide identified a number of key themes developed from a review of the relevant literature on haemoglobinopathies, chronic illness and ethnicity and welfare, discussions with key informants, advice from an 'expert' advisory committee and our own previous work, evaluating service support to parents of a child with SCD or thalassaemia (Atkin *et al.* 1998a, 1998b). Transcribed interviews were coded and indexed according to analytical themes and sub-themes. Following accepted conventions of qualitative analysis (Gubrium and Sliverman 1989), information was taken from the transcripts and transferred onto a map or framework, allowing comparison by theme and case. In writing up the findings, young people's responses were organized around four broad themes: living with a chronic illness; family relationships; coping strategies; and service delivery. This chapter explores one specific subject – use of medical regimens and precautions to reduce risk of complications, including during a painful crisis – which relates to all these themes. In the accounts below, pseudonyms are used to protect respondents' identities. Chapters 3 and 7 explore attribution of cause for haemoglobin disorders and parents' experiences of using services, respectively.

The findings

Managing sickle cell disorders

For many chronic illnesses, treatment regimens dominate the young person's life, often becoming the focal point for the difficulties of living with the condition (Mador and Smith 1989; Lemanek 1990; Hoare and Mann 1994; Atkin and Ahmad 2000). Medical regimens, however, do not usually have the same significance for many young people with SCD. Young people with thalassaemia, for example, often cited chelation therapy as the most difficult and disruptive aspect of their illness. Many go as far to say that they *hate* their treatment (Atkin and Ahmad in press). Such strong feelings were rare among those with SCD. The nature of medical treatment perhaps explains this. In thalassaemia, the injection of a drug, through a slow operating pump, eight to twelve hours a day, five to seven nights a week, cannot be compared with the oral medical regimens associated with SCD. Nor are the consequences of non-compliance comparable. Non-compliance with chelation therapy, in the case of thalassaemia major, results in premature death, whereas the consequence of non-compliance with medication, such as folic acid or penicillin, is less tangible. Precautions, such as keeping warm, avoiding too much physical exertion, drinking plenty of fluid and generally looking after oneself, can have a similarly nebulous effect. Consequently, the efficacy of the precautions is often not clear and compliance does not have the same significance as in other chronic illnesses such as thalassaemia, diabetes, severe asthma or cystic fibrosis.

Nonetheless, young people with SCD do find the need for constant medication and precautions disruptive. Non-compliance was therefore common and the reasons were similar to those given by young people with more demanding treatment regimens (Geiss *et al.* 1992; Atkin and Ahmad in press). However, those with SCD dealt with precautions and medication against a background of doubts about their efficacy; further, the potential dangers of non-compliance seemed too distant. Mandy Barnett (aged 19) explained why she did not take her folic acid and penicillin: 'Well it's not a matter of life or death is it?' Medical regimens had little legitimacy for many children. Having said this, young people did make judgements about the relative merits of different types of medication. This explained why all those prescribed hydroxyurea complied with their treatment. They felt that it did them good. Young people were also more likely to take penicillin than folic acid because they felt that it had more positive effects on their well-being. Mark Evans (aged 15), for instance, took his penicillin on a regular basis but often forgot about his folic acid: 'I must admit, I don't take folic acid. It does not seem important. But I always take my penicillin. I don't miss my penicillin because, like if I get a cold, I'd have it forever.'

Judgements about legitimacy also explain why young people are more likely to follow general precautions than comply with medical regimens. They feel precautions offer more protection from the painful crisis than medicine. Precautions derived particular importance from 'lived experience' becoming part of embodied knowledge about SCD. Several specifically remarked that only those with the illness could understand their needs and experiences. Don Gray (aged 13) emphasized the importance of looking after oneself. He added that this became easier over time as you learned what you can do and what you cannot do 'I've got to look after myself. I don't drive myself to the brink where like I'm out of breath. I'll take a breather, and not just carry on.'

Alvin Kanhai (aged 17) adopted a similar attitude:

> I just wouldn't get into any fights or anything that I'd have to, like sometimes I play football but not as often because sometimes if I've really like got out of breath, it might make my chest hurt. That happened the other day. It was only for a few hours but I just stay away from it.

Medical regimens did not have the same legitimacy, and this reflects young people's more ambivalent relationship to medical definitions of their illness. The episodic nature of the SCD, its unpredictability and variability among sufferers, undermined and discredited medical definitions (see also S.A. Hill 1994; Atkin and Ahmad 2000). Health professionals, for example, are not able to offer a definite prognosis nor definite advice on how to avoid a crisis. Medical regimens cannot guarantee well-being. Young people are therefore less reliant on medical discourses in making sense of their illness. To use them might even undermine their ability to cope (S.A. Hill 1994) as the young person is constantly faced by situations that cannot be explained by medical discourse and medical definitions can appear threatening. However, medical knowledge was never fully discredited. General precautions can also be undermined and this partially explained why they are not followed all the time, although – as we shall see – reasons for not following precautions are associated with the process of growing up.

The 'unfairness' of taking precautions and yet still experiencing complications also undermined their legitimacy. Several young people became especially dispirited if a crisis occurred even though they were taking the necessary precautions. Alvin Kanhai (aged 17) explained:

> I remember getting a crisis and I weren't doing nothing strenuous, and I weren't in the cold, and I wasn't doing nothing to bring it on. Basically I sat down and done nothing and I was still ill so I just couldn't do nothing to prevent it. That's what was making me so fed up with it. I mean, I don't know, what else are you supposed to do?

Nonetheless, young people do not feel that they can completely reject the need to follow precautions. Amina Daudji (aged 18) is dismissive of precautions but still feels that she has to follow them: 'No matter what I do if my crisis is going to come it will come. But I drink plenty of fluids and that can prevent it and I keep warm.'

Several young people rationalize this further by saying that they would have even more crises if they did not look after themselves. Gail Thomas (aged 13) follows precautions because she feels that they reduce the number of crises but she adds that it is sometimes difficult to stop the pain no matter what she does.

Thus, despite the young person's ambivalence, medical regimens and especially precautions are not entirely discredited. Young people are faced with an unpredictable illness and therefore need to feel that they can have some influence over the disease progression. Treatment and precautions offer a sense of personal control or *mastery* over their illness (also see S.A. Hill 1994). To feel wholly at the mercy of their illness and accept its pernicious nature would undermine a young person's sense of self. They have to have some hope of relief and 'hope' is an important resource in coming to terms with a chronic illness (Kliewer and Lewis 1995). This was especially evident during the painful crisis (see pp. 58–62). Taking medication and following precautions also enabled young people to keep the consequences of the illness separate from their self-image. They found this extremely valuable. To accept the unpredictability of the illness would be too destructive to cope with. Perceiving the illness as potentially controllable helped to maintain a valued self-image. This, however, created a constant tension in young people's lives. They knew from experience that medical regimens and precautions did not offer full protection against the consequences of the illness, while at the same time they had to exercise some control over disease progression. Young people were constantly balancing this tension and this explains why their response to treatment and precautions was constantly shifting. As we shall see, living with a chronic illness within the broad context of growing up further complicates this dynamic.

Age also appears to have an influence on compliance and the legitimacy it acquires. Those under 12, for example, tended to comply with medical regimens; parents usually assumed responsibility for their care and ensured they took their tablets. The older children, often responsible for their own medication, were less compliant. This was often informed by the young person's need to assert their own identity as well as the devaluing of medical regimens. We discuss this further below. Nor was there any return to medication, as the child grew older. This is in contrast to other chronic disorders, such as thalassaemia major where having faced the consequences of non-compliance, young people re-examine their attitude to regimes which help limit the effects of illness (Atkin and Ahmad in press). This rarely occurs in SCD and consequently, treatment regimens do not regain legitimacy as their effect on prognosis is variable. Precautions, however, may regain some legitimacy in relation to the growing child seeming to exercise some control over their condition.

The struggle associated with precautions tended to diminish with age. Young people begin to recognize the importance of working with the illness rather than against it. This is not to say that all older children have learnt to overcome the difficulties associated with SCD. Sadness, frustration and 'engulfment' can still occur and undermine strategies used to maintain normalcy and control, including taking precautions and medication. None-theless, those over 16 seemed better adjusted to the difficulties associated with their illness; a range of coping strategies enabled them to cope with the illness (see pp. 54–5).

Growing up with a chronic illness

Legitimacy, however, becomes informed by other, more symbolic influences affecting young people's relationship with illness (including precautions and medication) and general issues concerning growing up. To an extent, young people disliked medication and precautions because they mark out their difference rather than simply concerns about their efficacy. Their response was thus both emotional and rational (although we recognize that this distinction is not clear cut). Amina Daudji (aged 18) disliked taking medicines on a daily basis because 'It acknowledges the fact that I do have sickle cell, so I don't like taking them.'

Leroy Gordon (aged 15) often 'forgot' to take his medication: 'Because I try and lead a normal life as possible'. Lizzy Sol (aged 11) gets fed up taking medication. She felt that it was not 'normal': 'It's 'cos I just get sick of it. It was like my brother and my sister weren't taking tablets but I had to take them all my life and I didn't like, and I don't like them.'

General precautions were similarly viewed. Dawn Squires (aged 11) described how her mother made her wear a hat and gloves during the winter. She disliked this because she believed she looked out of place compared to her friends. Shirley Little (aged 12) noted that the need always to keep warm made her the 'odd one out'. Other girls felt that it was difficult to be as fashionable as their peers. Gail Thomas (aged 13) cannot wear the same short skirts because of the need to keep warm. This upset her and she felt left out, especially since she feared that people laughed at her behind her back.

Non-compliance, thus, represented a symbolic attempt at securing 'normality' within the broader context of growing up (see Lemanek 1990, in relation to asthma). Treatment and precautions become symbolic sites of strategy and struggle as young people attempt to assert their claims to self-determination and emphasize their similarity with peers. Three related themes inform this response.

First, as they grow older, young people are keen to assume adult roles, in the British context in the form of asserting their independence and own identity (Brannen *et al.* 1994; Frydenberg 1997). This can contribute directly to non-compliance among those with SCD, however, as they reject others' definitions of their problems, which is something noted for young people with chronic illness in general (Midence and Elander 1994; Atkin and Ahmad in press). As noted, non-compliance was especially high between the ages of 13 and 16, an age when status transition is being negotiated (Frydenberg 1997).

Second, and following on from the previous point, young people had to face the dilemma of how to reconcile a growing wish for independence with the threat of increased illness related dependence, a tension common among young people with a chronic illness (Sinnema 1992). This finds particular expression through their relationship with parents. Those over 13 especially felt dependent on their parents and unable to exercise the choices available to their peers. This is why, for instance, they disliked parental reminders about the value of medical regimens and precautions. Such tensions are common in other chronic illnesses such as cystic fibrosis, diabetes and thalassaemia (Mador and Smith 1989; Geiss *et al.* 1992; Atkin and Ahmad in press).

Third, older children found the regular need for medication and precautions restrictive and disruptive, preventing them from following – what they regard as – valued pursuits which would help emphasize their 'normality' and similarity with peers. Not being able to spend nights at friend's houses, as spontaneously as their peers, was noted by many as an indication of the restrictions of their illness. Bret Phillipson (aged 12) said that he had to take it easy and this meant he could not always go out with his friends. Alvin Kanhai (aged 17) explained how his illness set him aside from friends:

> When I was younger, when I went out with my friends they would be doing, they'd like run up and down and then I'd be like have to just follow them, like walk behind them, I couldn't really run too much because like I used to get just like, I'd wake up the next morning and the pain.

Such restrictions contributed to a sense of marginalization and isolation. Boys were more likely to bemoan the effects of precautions on their sporting activities, as noted by Mark Evans (aged 15): 'Because like normal people can play football; and nothing would happen to them, but if I do, I'll probably come back with a crisis.'

Coping with precautions and non-compliance with medical regimens

As we have seen, young people with SCD do not always value medical regimens and therefore have no difficulties in justifying non-compliance. Precautions, however, acquire greater legitimacy among young people but at the same time, they are aware of the emotional and symbolic difficulties caused by accepting the need for precautions. Balancing this tension is a particular problem for young people when they reach their teenage years. Consequently, the young persons were frustrated by the various demands precautions made on them, especially as they attempted to sustain a valued identity. Most were aware of the dilemma they faced in following precautions to maintain their well-being while at the same time attempting to limit the impact of their use on their self-identity. Achieving this balance is part of a dynamic process and explains why their responses to precautions (and to a lesser extent medical regimens) are constantly shifting and at times appear contradictory. As we have seen, attempting to exercise control over the illness, while at the same time being aware of the limitations of precautions and medical regimens, further informs this dynamic. This dynamic will also become apparent when we discuss the role of parents in negotiating responsibility for treatment.

Balancing the need to look after themselves and the need to limit the effect of the illness on self-image introduced another important feature of the young person's illness narrative: guilt. They were particularly guilty about the distress that non-compliance caused their parents, especially if they fell ill after ignoring their parents' advice. There were times, therefore, when young people admitted to pushing themselves too far. Becoming ill was often a potent reminder, that despite their ambivalence, they cannot fully reject precautions and medical regimens.

Young people also felt that they sometimes let their parents down. Their sense of guilt alongside a desire to avoid open conflict with parents partly explained why they disguised their non-compliance. Lizzy Sol (aged 11), for example, remarked that she always goes out of the house with her hat and gloves on but will take them off when she reaches the bus stop. This response represented a palatable form of non-conformity with parental wishes, where open challenge to parental authority is avoided (Drury 1991; Brannen *et al.* 1994).

Parents' own ambivalence towards medication and precautions (S.A. Hill 1994) was not recognized by young people (we return to this later; see also Chapter 7). Carol Prince (aged 15) often disregarded advice to keep warm but hid this from her mother: 'She would go up the wall if I told her.' Further, about half the young people told their parents they had taken their medication when they had not. Young people especially concealed non-compliance when they felt that it might have contributed to their painful crisis.

Another potential influence on medication and general precautions was young people's conception of reward and punishment. Those aged under

13 years especially felt that if they were 'good' they would not have a crisis. Taking precautions and following medical regimens could be related to this and become bound up with a more general idea of being a 'good' person. It would, therefore, be unjust if they experienced a crisis. Children may not be convinced fully by the benefits of treatment or precautions, but compliance could make them think they are being 'good'. Although not explicitly articulated in terms of religious values, such approaches do require some sense of an absolute being, beyond the immediate here and now, and a belief in divine justice (B.S. Turner 1987; Williams 1993).

The importance of successful adaptation to illness is increasingly being recognized (Beresford *et al.* 1996). There was no young person who was constantly overwhelmed by their illness, and few perceived illness as a 'destroyer' on a regular basis (see Herzlich 1973). Most young people, although aware that there were times when the illness took over their lives, attempted to ensure that SCD did not become a defining feature of their lives. Consequently, attempts to construct normality and reduce the impact of SCD on their life can only ever be partially successful. The severity and unpredictability of the illness provides too many reminders of the dangers and limitations they face. Young people are constantly juggling the difficulties associated with their condition and the possibility of relief from the consequences of their illness. The sadness at having SCD is greater during some periods than at other times. This is when they feel at the mercy of the illness and that the world is against them, a time when their sense of difference, anxiety, frustration and powerlessness was especially strong. Not only do treatment and precautions inform this estrangement, representing a symbolic reminder of the difficulties of living with SCD, but also their feelings of estrangement may affect compliance.

Negotiating responsibility: relationships with parents

Young people, as they seek to develop their own identities and establish 'normality', may reject their parents' or professionals' definitions of what is in their interests (see Mador and Smith 1989; S.A. Hill 1994; Frydenberg 1997). Treatment and precautions are often a focal point of these disagreements (Atkin *et al.* 1997). The parent–child relationship becomes fundamental in negotiating responsibility for compliance and gives specific expression to many of the issues discussed above.

Children under 12 are likely to follow precautions as they usually abide with the limits established by their parents. Few question the need for precautions or parental involvement. As children get older, however, and attempt to assert their independence, they are more likely to challenge parental and professional definitions of their needs. Precautions and to a lesser extent medical regimens lead to arguments with parents. Young people believe that their peers do not have to tolerate the same degree of parental 'interference'. Many also feel that the condition needlessly dominates their life because of their parents' concerns. Shirley Little (aged 12) explained:

'Because why, I mean, I can't do things like my friends. I want to go out with my friends and not have my mum there all the time.'

Most young people – of all ages and both sexes – feel that their parents are over-protective and prevent them from pursuing 'normal' activities. Gail Thomas (aged 12) falls out regularly with her parents: 'She [mother] says, like you can't wear shorts and all that stuff. You've got to keep warm. She always saying look after yourself. I say, "It isn't fair".' Leroy Gordon (aged 15) described his father as 'Mr Protective'. Leroy resented this and felt that he was old enough to take his own decisions. Several young people remarked that their parents still treated them as 'babies' and this annoyed them, as noted by Paula Grant (aged 11):

> I think I should be free like other children. OK, I've got sickle cell and when you've got sickle cell, it's like you are special, you can't do much things like other children can, but you can you know, sometimes. I don't think there's any reason why you can't go out without your coat on. She [mother] thinks I'm a baby. She doesn't listen to me.

Her mother's constant advice particularly annoyed Paula: 'You're thinking, hang on a sec, I'm not a baby. I'm 11 years old, for goodness sake. You know I do want to be respected.'

Young people found it difficult to talk to their parents about over-protectiveness. Compliance was felt to be imposed rather than negotiated. This made compliance more difficult to accept, although most attempted gradually to push back the boundaries and demonstrate their sense of responsibility to their parents. Parental trust had to be earned. Despite their frustration about over-protection, they usually understood their parents' concerns, as noted by Alvin Kanhai (aged 17) 'When she nags me about my tablets, I'd be like "well". It does get on my nerves a bit. But we're always, because we're a close family and everything, we don't really argue. It's like my mother says it because it's good for me and that's it.'

Many young people similarly commented that their parents acted only out of love for them. Shirley Little (aged 12) remarked: 'Sometimes they [her parents] care a bit too much, I think. But only because they love me.' Most young people, therefore, saw parental intervention as well intentioned; however, this did not necessarily mean that it made dealing with parents any easier. Acknowledgement of parental concerns and need to establish their own sense of autonomy added to the young people's confusion and made them feel guilty about arguing with their parents, even when they thought they had a just cause. This understanding is again caught up with the young people's constantly shifting response to their illness. Consequently, there are times when young people are more understanding than others. Our previous work also suggests there are times when parents are more conscious of non-compliance than others and this is reflected in their relationship with the child (Atkin *et al.* 1997).

The parents' response was not without its ambivalence, although this was not always recognized by the child. These parents seemed less assertive in ensuring compliance compared to parents of children who had thalassaemia. This may reflect the difference in the nature of the two conditions or differences in family values between African Caribbean and Asian families. Parents tended to share their child's scepticism about the value of medical regimens and consequently, compared to thalassaemia, treatment regimens *per se* were a less frequent source of tension when the child has SCD. And compared to parents whose children had thalassaemia (Atkin and Ahmad in press), these parents seemed more prepared to entrust medical and more general precautions to their older children while retaining this responsibility for younger children.

Several young people, however, noted that their parents were no longer explicitly telling them what to do, while reminding them that they would be responsible for any adverse affects from not following precautions. Amina Daudji (aged 18) described how she fell out with her father when she was taken ill:

> When I fall ill my dad will say to me it's because, you know, you didn't take your medication, and we have a lot of arguments about that and then he goes, 'It's for your benefit, it's for you. It does not make a difference to me if you take them or not, you know'. So we do argue a lot.

Alvin Kanhai (aged 17) remarked that his mother adopted a similar approach: 'I suppose she does not go on as much as she used to. For the past year, she just say, "well it's your fault if you're sick" and that's it'.

Feeling guilty
Young people often express guilt at not taking medications and precautions, and for arguing with their parents; parents sometimes exploit this to emphasize the value of precautions. It was rare, however, for young people to blame parents for the inherited nature of the condition, despite it being a concern of many parents. Nor do they use non-compliance as a way of getting back at their parents. If blame did emerge it was often during a painful crisis. Four young people – three girls and one boy – said that they blamed their parents for the illness when they were in pain, something they later regretted. Gail Thomas (aged 13), for example, remarked: 'I hate them [parents] for it. I don't mean it. When I'm in pain, I always blame it on them. It's all your fault why I've got it. But I shouldn't do it really.' Gail tried to avoid talking to her mother about the illness when she was sad, because she would end up arguing with her mother: 'All I would say is it's all your fault. So it's best I keep it to myself'. Gail would not, however, advise others to blame their parents: 'I might say, right my mum's for it but I says don't hurt your mother because without her you wouldn't be here.'

More generally, most children admitted there were times when they took out the frustrations associated with their illness on their parents. Again, this appears to be a key feature of growing up with a chronic illness (Geiss *et al.* 1992). Young people, for example, admitted there were times when they were 'awful' to their parents. They recognized they can be 'grumpy' and 'moody', often using their parents as scapegoats for the problems associated with SCD.

Managing the painful crisis

Up to now this chapter has largely focused on young people's response to their treatment during the illness's 'steady state'. For many sufferers and their families, the painful crisis is often the defining feature of SCD, symbolic of the difficulties associated with the illness (Midence and Elander 1994). Medication becomes caught up in this and acquires particular significance when the child is in pain. This included daily medication and precautions, as well as the specific administration of analgesics. As part of this, the onset of the painful crisis created a different set of circumstances with which the young person and their families had to cope. The painful crisis required a practical and emotional response that was quite different from coping with the everyday consequences of SCD. Young people's ability to separate these two aspects of the illness could emerge as an important aspect of their coping strategy. The disruptive aspects and emotional consequences of the painful crisis, for example, could be minimized as the young person attempted to focus on coping with the everyday consequences of the illness. Most recognized, for instance, the value of not letting worries about the pain dominate their life. Nonetheless, the distinction between the two dimensions of the illness could never be total. At times, the painful crisis can be seen as one aspect of the illness; at other times, it symbolizes the illness. The young person's illness narrative can simultaneously reflect both positions. More generally, the possibility of the painful crisis contributed to the vulnerability of young people's coping strategies and introduced a sense of uncertainty. To this extent, they had to deal with not only the consequences of pain but also the possibility of pain.

Daily medication and precautions are bound up with this. The fear of pain is a powerful influence on compliance, although not all young people complied with routine medication and precautions. Instrumental use of precautions was common. For example, compliance improved when young people feared an impending crisis, or when they were confronted with important events – birthdays, exams, Christmas – during which they were particularly keen to remain healthy.

With the onset of pain, there is a change in young people's response to treatment. Whatever their ambivalence during the illness's steady state, they now fully embrace medical intervention. This is seen to offer the only possible relief from the pain. Young people realize from experience that it is important not to ignore the onset of pain. They begin to take it easy and start taking painkillers. They also try to take their mind off the pain by focusing on other activities: reading, watching television, playing computer games and socializing with friends. Alvin Kanhai (aged 17), for example, said: 'I would just do anything to forget'. However, the fear of an impending major crisis makes it difficult to 'forget' the pain. Many, for example, look for signs that the pain is going to go away but are then filled with despair as they realize a major crisis is developing. This is when young people are at their most vulnerable. Pain can, therefore, evoke a real fear as well as a sense of panic. Bret Phillipson's (aged 12) illness narrative reflected this and he described his initial response to the pain: 'I go crazy. Start running around thinking what to do.'

To avoid worrying parents, many young people are often reluctant to tell their parents when they are in pain, especially during the early stages of a crisis. Several remarked, for instance, that their parents would not know of all of the minor crises they have experienced. Guilt again emerges as part of the illness narrative. Young people are concerned about their parents' distress and realize that parents find pain difficult to cope with; this is especially evident to those over 15 years old. Leroy Gordon (aged 15) explained why he kept the pain to himself for as long as possible: 'I don't want to upset her [mother]. So I try and keep it to myself.' Ellie Gordon (aged 16), for example said she knows that her parents are upset when she in pain but feels helpless because there is nothing she can do about it. Parents' accounts confirm these feelings of distress and helplessness when their child is in pain (Atkin *et al.*, Chapter 7 in this volume). Young people also worry about the disruptions that their crisis causes for family life. Leroy Gordon (aged 15) pointed out that a painful crisis affects all aspects of family life: 'It kind of disrupts everything because like, my little bother has got to be picked up from school and my mother, she has work, so does me dad. They have to visit me in hospital.'

Guilt, or a desire to protect loved ones, was not the only reason for disguising the pain. Several young people felt that their parents would overreact if they mentioned the pain. Amina Daudji (aged 18) remarked that her parents worried too much when she was unwell; a painful crisis heightened these concerns. Amina therefore had learnt from experience not to mention 'minor pains': 'They [parents] just take over my life. They do everything for me and tell me what not to do. I hate it. When they fuss over me, that really annoys me.'

Many young people especially disliked drawing attention to their illness or being reminded of their difference. Mentioning the pain undermined this as their parents assumed a more proactive caring role. However, as we shall see, the intensity of the pain made greater parental involvement inevitable. In a few cases, young people said that they would not mention their pain if they had gone against their parents' advice and not followed precautions. Andrew Little (aged 12), for example, would keep his pain secret if he had been outside without his coat. He felt that his parents would be annoyed with him for not keeping warm and he could do without the 'hassle'.

With the onset of a major crisis, young people become overwhelmed by their illness and everyday coping strategies begin to break down. They can no longer keep their illness at a distance. The crisis specifically reintroduces concerns and anxieties about their future with young people feeling powerless and helpless in view of the severity of their illness and its impact on their life. Gail Thomas (aged 13) described her response to the pain: 'Sometimes I feel like, just to be dead and all that. Because like being in crisis you really can't take the pain, you just want it to be over . . . I wouldn't wish it on nobody else.'

At the same time as feeling overwhelmed by SCD, many attempted to be positive. This again illustrates the importance of hope in making sense of chronic illness. Young people attempted to come through the pain by reminding themselves that it will not go on forever: 'And like when I'm sick, it'll be gone in a week, that what I think' (Antony John, aged 15).

Young people also started to rely more on their parents during a major crisis. This contrasted with their strategy during the steady state or during mild pain, where they limited their dependence on parents. Alvin Kanhai (aged 17), for example, said it was one of the few times he was dependent on his mother: 'It's like I only need her when I'm like, I've got a crisis and she's always there anyway. She just supports me and talks to me about things, it just, she's always there so I've never had to worry.'

Such reliance does not seem to undermine the personal maintenance of a positive self-image – at least in the short term. Young people also depended on their parents' response to legitimize their 'sick role' and more specifically the use of painkillers. By adopting a caring role, parents recognized that the child's concerns are real. This is especially important given the uncertainties associated with SCD.

In more practical terms, all young people praised their parents' involvement and support during the painful crisis. Many remarked that parents were the best people to have around when they were in pain. Gail Thomas's (aged 13) account was typical: 'She [mother] helped me through it. She's always there for me.' Management of pain often involved the whole family. Mothers usually assumed the main responsibilities for care and take on a range of activities. They ensured that the child was comfortable, gave reassurance and encouragement, and administered pain relief. Fathers became involved by undertaking support activities for the mother. Fathers were also praised for activities such as massaging the child as well as talking them through the pain, as noted by Mark Evans (aged 15): 'He just, either rubs it for me until I go to sleep or talks to me about it. Sometimes when I am poorly, he just say, "Son, just forget about it and relax", you know put it in a way that will not hurt me as much.'

Most young people recognized that their parents tried hard to stay calm and disguise their sadness, but remarked that their parents' attempts were never entirely successful. Mark Evans (aged 15), for example, said his mother tried to hide her tears when he was in pain: 'But I can tell it from my mum's face.' Gail Thomas (aged 13) was upset by the effect of her painful crisis on her mother: 'She gets so upset when I'm having a pain and it's not fair on her, like I don't want to make her worry. Because if she's upset I get upset for upsetting her.'

Young people, especially as they grow older, have to deal with not only their own response to the pain, but also their parents' response.

Administering analgesics

Painkillers prescribed for use at home can be only partially successful during a major crisis; young people usually have to be hospitalized. However, most – especially those over 15 – would go to hospital only as a last resort. They remained ambivalent about hospital admission, perhaps more so than their parents (see Atkin *et al.*, Chapter 7).

As a reflection of young people's reliance on parents during a crisis, most, irrespective of their age, allowed parents to decide when it is time to go into hospital. In four cases – all boys over 16 – hospital admission was negotiated with parents.

Young people's experience of pain control in hospitals, however, was not wholly positive. In the first instance, many of the older young people berated the hospital's procedures; a variety of problems were noted. One-third of the sample were required to go to the casualty department before they could be allocated a hospital bed, despite it being contrary to national policy guidance (Standing Medical Aduisory Committee (SMAC) 1994). This often led to a delay in pain relief. Young people found this especially difficult to deal with because they recognized the opportunity of adequate pain control on the ward but in the mean time had to suffer with little or no relief. Waiting for up to three hours in the accident and emergency department before admission to a ward was common. Mandy Barnett (aged 19) described her experience: 'You have to wait around, that was the worst because it was the pain and because I've got sickle cell I should have been put in a ward straight away rather than wait around. I mean it was one and half hours last time.'

Many young people also commented that doctors working in casualty were ignorant about sickle cell. Alvin Kanhai (aged 17) said: 'I think the doctors in casualty, well the one that was treating me, I don't think he really knew about sickle cell anyway.' As we shall see, this ignorance often continues once the child is admitted to the ward. Our previous work showed that parents also found the health professionals' ignorance distressing; parents' and children's own knowledge and experiences were often discounted by the professionals (see Atkin *et al.*, Chapter 7).

Lack of knowledge among nursing staff and junior doctors emerged as an ongoing problem and was especially apparent to older children. Several young people, for example, took charge of their treatment because they felt that some of the nursing staff were incapable of looking after them adequately. They expected a high degree of competence and resented having to educate doctors and nurses, especially when they were in pain. Young people were also critical of doctors' arrogant and patronizing attitude, which often accompanied this ignorance. Sharon Francis (aged 19) commented: 'And like, they're dead funny and stand-offish and because they're doctors, think they know it all, and, they don't really.' The arrogance of hospital staff who believe that they know more than the young person, when they obviously did not, was a common theme in the child's illness narrative, and something also noted in the parents' accounts (see Atkin *et al.*, Chapter 7).

Professionals' social skills were important in young people and their parents having a positive experience of hospital treatment (see also Chamba *et al.* 1999). Once on the ward, young people's relationship with hospital staff was mixed. Gail Thomas's (aged 13) experience was typical. She remarked that some nurses were supportive: 'Say like you're in pain then they try and like talk to you and they say it's going to be over soon and stuff like that. They just comfort you.' There was one especially supportive nurse: 'Because she just was, when I was crying she always used to come to me and hug me and kiss me, yeah she just really was nice.' Gail, however, had problems with other nurses. 'I remember some of them. Some of them were a bit snobby, didn't know how to work with children by the looks of things . . . Because you can see it in their faces . . . And some of the nurses are too busy. They don't have a clue.' She described her problems with one particular nurse: 'She doesn't really smile at you. Like she can be really bossy to you. Like saying, you have to get up and walk because it helped you, even when you're in pain. She tried to say get up and stop being lazy, that sort of stuff.'

Emma Hardin (aged 16) similarly remarked that some nurses were better than others. She described how several nursing staff would make her feel welcome and reassure her when she was in pain. Others would ignore her: 'They always say "wait there" and then come half an hour later.'

Another common theme was hospital staff's insensitivity to the young person's pain. This is a feature of previous research (Maxwell and Streetly 1998) and parents' accounts (Atkin *et al.*, Chapter 7). Young people complained about their pain not being taken seriously with some hospital staff feeling that they exaggerated the pain. This, at a time of great distress, greatly offended them. For example, Amina Daudji (aged 18) noted: 'Because they should understand you better, understand what kind of pain you're having, what you're going through.'

Alvin Kanhai (aged 17) described some nurses as 'nasty': 'They are really quite nasty. They say like stupid things, "Oh, be quiet. You're not really as bad as you say." But as I got older, because I was in so much pain I'd shout at them and just tell them to shut up because they don't really know.'

Many young people described instances where they felt that the nurses deliberately ignored their distress. Leroy Gordon (aged 15) described a recent incident when he could not get the attention of nursing staff: 'So I rang the buzzer and there was five nurses on, on ward and it took 'em, I think it was, 20 to 30 minutes to come. They were too busy watching TV. I buzzed at the wrong time. They were all watching *Emmerdale*.'

Discussion

The debate about the use of treatment regimens among young people with a chronic illness is frequently unsophisticated (Lenney *et al.* 1994). It fails to fully appreciate how individuals and their families relate to their treatment as they attempt to make sense of the illness within the context of personal circumstances, identities, lifestyles and coping strategies (Ahmad and Atkin 1996a). Following this, health professionals sometimes fail to recognize how young people and their families manage their treatment and, consequently, are unable to give appropriate support (Anderson *et al.* 1985). There are, for example, basic misunderstandings about the purpose and importance of treatment between professionals and children (and their carers) (Johnson 1988). This is regrettable since timely and appropriate support can facilitate coping, including enhanced compliance with regimes which limit complications (Midence 1994).

Facilitating successful illness management, therefore, must begin with understanding the illness experience of those receiving the treatment and their social context. This gives primacy to the individual's experience and is a reminder that medical treatment is not merely a technical exercise. Medical treatments as well as lifestyle precautions are constructed and interpreted by the individuals, reflecting the shifting relationships between illness, body and self as well as social relationships (Bury 1991). The individual's experience, therefore, should not be subordinated to medical discourse in which they are seen as a body to be transformed and improved (Atkin 1991).

Emphasizing the primacy of individual experience is especially important for young people. The need to involve them in decisions about their care has led to numerous policy documents and much practice guidance (World Health Organization (WHO) 1989; Social Services Inspectorate 1994a, 1994b). Many service interventions fail, because they have not adequately addressed young people's views and/or apply strategies derived from 'adult' frameworks (International Planned Parenthood Federation 1992). Investigating the views of young people thus becomes important in providing a more sophisticated account of how they understand, experience and cope with their illness, as well as in the development of appropriate and accessible provision (Brannen *et al.* 1994).

Exploring young people's response to treatment demonstrates the complexity of their illness narrative. Perhaps not surprisingly, young people's responses to medical regimens and precautions went through phases and were subject to individual variability. Difficulties, however, were rarely associated with the practical activity of following treatment or precautions but were bound up with their everyday experience of living with a chronic illness. Compliance also becomes informed by the more general problems of coping with the new experiences and responsibilities of growing up. These two interrelated themes represent an important starting point in understanding medical treatment and lifestyle changes and seem relevant to other chronic conditions such as severe asthma, diabetes, cystic fibrosis and thalassaemia (Stark *et al.* 1987; Midence 1994; Klinnert 1997; Atkin and Ahmad in press).

Medical regimens become part of the wider process in which young people make sense of their illness (Bury 1991). Medical regimens and precautions, for example, were seen as marking out a young person's difference from their peers. This became especially apparent to children between the ages of 13 and 16, a period of role transition when compliance is often at its worst. To this extent, rejection of compliance can be seen as an attempt at securing normality, expressing choice and negating the most obvious symbol of difference within the broader context of growing up. As a consequence, young people are constantly trying to balance the value of precautions to their well-being, while at the same time coming to terms with the emotional difficulties caused by its use. Young people with other chronic illnesses seem to face similar dilemmas (Johnson 1988), although in the case of SCD, young people express doubts about the value of the medical regimens they are expected to follow. This created a further tension in the young person's life. Young people knew from experience that medical regimens and precautions did not offer full protection against the consequences of the illness, while at the same time feeling they had to exercise some control over the disease.

These balancing processes are dynamic and explain why the response to compliance is constantly shifting. Compliance, although poor among the 13–16 age group, still remained varied between individuals and with the same individual over time. There are times when they comply well and others when compliance is poor. This balance is further influenced by the young person's coping strategies, an increasingly important aspect of understanding the experience of those with a chronic illness (Beresford *et al.* 1996). Most coping strategies are generally vulnerable and there are occasions when young people are overwhelmed by the difficulties they face. Not surprisingly, this is reflected in their response to precautions. The greater the sense of being overwhelmed, the more likely the rejection of treatment and precautions.

Besides this, family relationships offer another dimension to the young people's illness narratives and represent the context for their relationship with illness and its consequences (Sloper and Turner 1992). 'Overprotectiveness' often becomes part of this debate as young people feel that their parents overemphasize the need for precautions, thus limiting choices enjoyed by their peers. Nonetheless, this is not to say that young people do not acknowledge their parents' concerns and they often experience guilt for not following precautions. They are particularly guilty about the distress that their non-compliance caused their parents. This guilt in turn increases their difficulties of coming to terms with SCD and can undermine their coping strategies, which then increases the chance of non-compliance.

The genetic basis of SCD does not seem to inform a young person's response to medical regimens and – more generally – was not usually a feature of their illness narrative. Indeed, their response to compliance was similar to that of young people with conditions as diverse as severe asthma (Lemanek 1990), cystic fibrosis (Geiss *et al.* 1992), rheumatoid arthritis (Anderson *et al.* 1985) and diabetes (Johnson 1988). Nor was gender implicated in the treatment process despite some evidence suggesting that girls might be better equipped to cope with the emotional demands of medical regimens than boys (see Frydenberg 1997). In this study, for example, girls were just as likely as boys not to take precautions.

The onset of pain, however, could create a different set of circumstances with which the young person had to cope. In the first instance the possibility of the painful crisis contributed to the vulnerability of young people's coping strategies, reminding them of the uncertainties associated with their illness. Young people can worry about the pain even when they are well and it represents a constant reminder of their fragile claims to 'normality'. The onset of pain also represents a change in young people's response to treatment. Whatever their ambivalence during the illness's 'steady state', they now fully embrace medical discourse and intervention; this is seen to offer the only possible relief from the pain. The severity of the pain also means that many young people are aware of the immediate benefits of pain relief administered in hospital. Young people's experience of pain control in hospitals is not wholly positive, however, and many report problems in adequate treatment of pain. Particular problems include delays in treatment of pain, as well as ignorance and insensitivity of health professionals. These appear long-standing problems in the treatment of pain among those with SCD (Black and Laws 1986; Murray and May 1988; Anionwu 1993; Midence 1994; Midence and Elander 1994; Maxwell and Streetly 1998).

Institutional racism plays an important part in making sense of these problems (Ahmad and Atkin 1996a). The ignorance of health professionals is often attributed to identification of SCD with 'black' communities. The NHS has been extremely slow to recognize haemoglobinopathies as significant public health issues (Anionwu 1996b). Those endeavouring to improve services, for example, have difficulties competing with the more 'traditional' concerns of the NHS, used to catering for the needs of a predominantly white population (Bradby 1996; Dyson 1998). Pain relief as well as ongoing support for sufferers and carers becomes caught up in this neglect. This neglect is further informed by stereotypes suggesting that minority ethnic patients have a lower pain threshold (Ahmad et al. 1991; Bowler 1993) and may mean that health professionals underestimate the young person's pain. Lack of treatment can also be justified by another racial myth. As we have seen, people with SCD require powerful drugs for the control of pain. Some doctors, however, worry about their African Caribbean patients becoming dependent on drugs (Stimmel 1993). More generally, as Hurtig (1994) has pointed out, the medical myth is that pain in SCD is 'manipulative' and can 'serve to demand attention at best and drugs at worst'. There is no evidence to suggest that addiction to powerful pain killing drugs is a significant problem among SCD sufferers (Midence and Elander 1994). The racist assumptions contribute to the poor pain relief for people during a painful crisis and mean that perhaps the most distressful aspect of their illness remains under-treated (SMAC 1994).

Conclusion

Young people's response to medical regimens and precautions is both complex and dynamic. The everyday experience of living with a chronic illness, the general difficulties of growing up, and family relationships are all implicated in the compliance process. This means that their rejection of treatment and precautions was rarely associated with practical difficulties but more informed by an emotional response, as they attempted to maintain a valued self-image and assert their growing sense of personal autonomy. Their experiences and responses have much in common with those of young people with other serious chronic illnesses (Stark *et al.* 1987; Hayford and Ross 1988; Lemanek 1990; Geiss *et al.* 1992; Klinnert 1997). And for these young people, living with SCD must be seen against the backdrop of simply being a young person (Brannen *et al.* 1994; Frydenberg 1997).

Acknowledgements

Our grateful thanks to the young people and their families for their time and hospitality, the National Lottery Charities Board for generous funding, Kanwal Mand for help with interviews, the many professionals who assisted with the study, and our Young Persons' Reference Group and the Advisory Committee for sound guidance.

5

'I send my child to school and he comes back an Englishman': minority ethnic deaf people, identity politics and services

Waqar I.U. Ahmad, Aliya Darr and Lesley Jones

Much has been written on and by Deaf people (Ahmad *et al.* 1998: ch. 3).[1] In particular, a reconceptualization of deafness has been offered, akin to the critique of the medical approach to conceptualization of disability. However, Deaf people and many hearing researchers (see for example Lane 1993; Lane *et al.* 1996) have argued against their incorporation as disabled people. Deaf identity is constructed on the grounds of having a shared language (in the case of Britain, the British Sign Language – BSL) and the experience of shared oppression from a hearing world. Many argue that the status of Deaf people is that of a 'linguistic minority' within British society. There is an ongoing debate between proponents of the social model of disability and those of a political model of deafness (see Ahmad *et al.* 1998: ch. 3; Corker 1998). Some have accused deaf people of being disablist for refusing to build alliances with people with other forms of 'impairment'. Some in the Deaf movement feel marginalized by disabled activists, who impose a disabled identity on Deaf people. This is a necessarily simplistic summary of often complex arguments; the reader can follow up the debates elsewhere (Lane 1993; Ahmad *et al.* 1998; Corker 1998).

In much of the literature on Deaf people, ethnic diversity within Deaf people remains unacknowledged. There is little recognition of people's legitimate claims to having multiple identities. The fact that minority ethnic Deaf people may experience racist marginalization within the Deaf community is rarely addressed. Since the early 1990s, however, some literature has emerged on the lives and experiences of minority ethnic Deaf people (Sharma and Love 1991; Badat and Whall-Roberts 1994). Our own work in this field has focused on Deaf people themselves as well as their families and services (Aliya Darr *et al.* 1997; Ahmad *et al.* 1998; Chamba *et al.* 1998a,

1998b). This chapter focuses on issues concerning identity and ethnicity in the lives of minority ethnic Deaf people.

Construction, maintenance and celebration of identity through organized activity is an important aspect of the lives of minority ethnic deaf people (Ahmad *et al.* 1998). Among the variety of initiatives on ethnicity and deafness identified by Ahmad *et al.* (1998), those which are user led largely concentrate on social, cultural and religious issues and can be seen in terms of a quest for discovering and strengthening identities other than those defined by their deafness. Here we discuss these initiatives in depth and explore issues of identity politics and its links with a range of self-help-based voluntary and statutory sector initiatives.

A number of important issues in relation to construction and negotiation of identities in the lives of minority ethnic Deaf people are explored in this chapter. First, the importance of religion and culture from the perspectives of young people, their parents and workers is addressed, including the attempts which are made to instil religious and cultural values in deaf children and the problems faced in doing this successfully. Second, the emergence of social and cultural groups is explored in terms of their focus, organization and value to users. These groups raise interesting questions about multiple identities (based on deafness, gender, religion and ethnicity) and their negotiation. The diversity of responses to identity politics parallels that found in the wider literature on ethnicity and identity (Drury 1991; Modood *et al.* 1994). Third, the importance of learning and networking through various initiatives is traced, addressing how this empowers and informs people, facilitates supportive networks and enables improved communication between families and their deaf members. Fourth, we focus on some developments in mainstream services aimed at making them more ethnically sensitive, although as we shall see, this does not constitute a marked cultural shift in mainstream services. Finally, we discuss various respondents' perspectives on the need for 'specialist' provision, although we use this term loosely; here, deaf counselling and sign language interpreting are discussed in particular.

The study

We identified 104 initiatives with deaf people from minority ethnic communities. Data were collected through networking with deaf groups and organizations, a fact-finding workshop with deaf professionals and other participants from minority ethnic groups, requests in deaf and ethnic minority media for information and a systematic postal survey of the following agencies in England and their equivalents in Scotland, Wales and Northern Ireland: social services departments; district health authorities; regional health authorities; NHS trusts; local education authorities; known deaf clubs and organizations; race equality councils; community health councils; Family Health Service Authorities; and councils for voluntary services. The postal survey was supplemented by the use of video, telephone (text as well as voice) and face to face interviews.

Face to face interviews were conducted with people involved with a range of initiatives as users, workers or in other capacities. In choosing initiatives for detailed interviews, we wished to reflect the diversity of initiatives in terms of geographical concentration, target group (ethnicity, gender, deaf or hard of hearing), sectoral base (voluntary, statutory) and funding (relatively secure initiatives as well as those with little secure funding). Where appropriate, we interviewed workers, users and line managers. For example, for a youth club, we interviewed the youth worker, the line manager responsible for continued funding and four club members. Topic guides were used for loosely structured discussion. In total 85 interviews were conducted. Of these, 45 were with 'providers' (workers, line managers, volunteers), 37 with users and 4 with researchers. Overall, 45 respondents were deaf and 40 were hearing. Most interviews were done individually but some were conducted in groups. A number of different languages were used with deaf respondents:

- a Deaf interviewer using British Sign Language with Deaf BSL users
- a hearing interviewer with a BSL interpreter with Deaf people
- a hearing interviewer using sign-supported English with deaf people
- spoken English with oral deaf people.

Hearing respondents were interviewed in English, Urdu, Punjabi, Gujarati and Bengali (last two with interpreters). The range of languages and approaches used allowed respondents to use their preferred language.

All interviews with hearing respondents and with Deaf respondents using sign language interpreters were audio-recorded; those using BSL were video-recorded. The interviews in BSL and in spoken languages other than English were translated. Full transcripts were used for analysis.

'I send my child to school and he comes back an Englishman': concerns about religious and cultural socialization

Parents found it particularly difficult to convey aspects of their cultural and religious background to their children and many were concerned that their children knew more about the 'British' way of life than their own cultural values and traditions. Parents not using BSL or for the oral children, the children not having access to their home language, resulted in poor communication between deaf children and their families. This led to frustrations on both sides. A Bengali bilingual worker who had close contact with Bengali deaf children talked about the tensions faced by the parents she visited:

They [the parents] find it [culture and religion] extremely difficult to explain and they live in a western society. Whereas they want to hold onto their traditions and things but they can't because they can't explain things to them and if they argue too much they end up fighting and then the kids will want to go and leave home and things.

Even when deaf children had acquired a basic understanding of their religion from their parents, all too often they were not provided with adequate explanations for these religious beliefs. This was largely because many parents and children shared no common language in which to communicate complex concepts. As a result of limited access to information, many deaf children grew up with rigid ideas about their religion with little understanding of the underlying philosophies or scope for negotiation of religious observance. Other work shows that individuals utilize culture and religion as flexible resources, allowing considerable scope to negotiate values and lifestyles (Drury 1991; Modood *et al.* 1994; Ahmad 1996). The inherent contradictions and differences within cultures provide opportunities for challenging certain definitions of norms. However, the ability to successfully negotiate behaviour depends on individual position and possession of cultural capital. Many respondents, Deaf and hearing, argued that the poor communication between deaf children or young people and their families, and the relative marginalization of Deaf people within their wider ethnic and religious communities, afford them few opportunities to accumulate such cultural capital. They are, therefore, less able to negotiate norms and behaviours without causing offence or conflict. One Asian sign language interpreter explained her view of how ideas about religion were internalized by the Deaf person:

> if you look at hearing Asian people, yeah, you hear something and then you think, ignore it, because you know it's nonsense, you know, you must tie your hair up because, whatever and you know it's . . . your choice. Well with deaf people, because they don't have, um . . . access to that wider debate, if you see what I mean, if you tell them something, that is it and they have to do it that way.

An Asian deaf outreach worker extended this problem to lack of knowledge about other areas of life, such as marriage functions:

> I've met lots of Asian deaf people who don't understand what a dowry is . . . They don't understand that issue at all. They don't know the language so they don't understand what it means that way . . . they don't understand why the wedding is large. They don't understand anything about the marriage ceremonies or anything, the dowries, they don't even understand that, it's a very basic thing. I think it's a problem.

This is not to claim that all Deaf people find it difficult to function successfully as full members of their religious and ethnic communities. However, we must acknowledge that their marginalization, by the hearing family and community members, limits their chances to acquire the cultural knowledge and skills regarded as normal for their hearing peers. For example, a

Jewish deaf young man, having grown up as part of the Jewish hearing community, recalled occasions on which deaf people were excluded from joining in religious festivities such as bar mitzvahs: 'I knew nothing as a child about my culture except that there was something about music but that was not available to me. I became aware that there was different food, but at school I had only English food.'

The neglect of minority ethnic languages, cultures, histories and religions in school education is well recognized (Cashmore and Troyna 1990). It is a particular issue in the education of minority ethnic deaf children (Chamba et al. 1998a). Not surprisingly, many respondents felt that schools were doing little to provide information about minority religions and cultures, although some were making attempts to plug this gap. One school for deaf children had invited a hearing voluntary worker to address school assemblies on Islam. This Pakistani man had good signing skills and a strong commitment to promoting greater religious awareness among the younger deaf people:

> I think it's a big issue for the younger Deaf Asian community. Where can we get teachings or understanding or awareness about our way of life, or our family's way of life, or our parents' way of life? Because they can't get it at school, they certainly can't get it at home, they can't read it in a book and they can't watch a video because there isn't any videos on it . . . I think that's lacking as well. I've not seen very much of it being provided. I think that would be across the board whether it's from Social Services or from the Health Authority, none of them's providing it and education's not providing it either.

Such neglect, coupled with the parents' own limited ability to provide cultural socialization in the way they provide for hearing children, led many parents to fear losing their deaf children to a Deaf 'white culture' (see Anwar 1977; Ahmad 1996, for discussion of parental concerns regarding cultural reproduction). Anwar (1977) notes that parents employ strategies both to instil their cultural values in children and to safeguard against adoption of the wider society's values. Parental ability to employ either of these strategies with their deaf children was compromised. The fear that their deaf children will lose their ethnic and religious identity is powerfully summed up by a Bangladeshi mother: 'I send my child to school and he comes back an Englishman.'

To combat these perceived problems, a Pakistani mother who had learnt basic signing had decided to write to a deaf organization in Pakistan, for materials on religious education. In contrast, a group of Bengali mothers had approached their local National Deaf Children's Society to request suitable provision to cater for the cultural and religious needs of their teenage Deaf children.

It was usually only after finishing compulsory schooling that many Deaf young people realized their relative lack of knowledge about their own ethnicity, history and culture; this was a cause of regret and resentment to many but the process of rediscovering and reclaiming cultural and religious identities was also empowering. For example, one Indian origin Deaf woman was now trying to reaffirm her cultural identity:

> I never really considered myself as an Asian person. I was very ashamed to wear bangles and I was very ashamed to wear saris . . . I think in the past, I fooled myself in the past. Really I think it has taken me 15 years to reach where I am today. Now I feel much more positive.

However, not having been taught any Hindi as a child, she felt excluded from aspects of Indian culture and history.

The cultural isolation of African Caribbean young people was felt to be particularly acute. Accessible written materials on African and Caribbean people were thought to be lacking, their needs were often subsumed under those of white deaf people, and there was a severe shortage of African Caribbean Deaf role models. A Deaf African Caribbean youth worker highlighted the need for accessible information on African and Caribbean histories, cultures, arts and literature: 'Black and Asian hearing people have their own magazines which incorporates their culture and history, everything, it's beautiful. There is nothing historical for black, Deaf people.' Further, the perceived lack of Deaf African Caribbean role models was felt to make it harder for young African Caribbean Deaf people to develop and sustain a positive ethnic identity.

Having gained only a limited understanding of their own ethnic identity, it is not surprising that many deaf children from minority ethnic communities had grown up with confused notions of their ethnic and religious identity and relationships with the wider society. For many, it appeared only natural that they should see themselves first and foremost as Deaf people, belonging to the Deaf community, albeit a predominantly white Deaf community. Some members of an Asian Deaf youth group, we interviewed, felt that sharing a common language (BSL) made it easier for minority ethnic Deaf people to identify with white Deaf people rather than with hearing members of their own ethnic and religious community:

> Asian [Deaf] women were more closer to Deaf community than to anybody else because they're Deaf first and then Asian . . . I think Deaf, it's all different really, Deaf community is Deaf first then Asian because even for the Asian Deaf their way of communication is via BSL, [or] in English, so they're more happy to use their (communication) skills with a Deaf person rather than an Asian family who doesn't communicate.

Communication thus affected networks and the ability to function effectively as a full member of a community. For this respondent, the shared communication with other Deaf people, irrespective of ethnicity, ensured the strength of ties with other Deaf people. Equally, limited communication with their hearing ethnic group family members and peers weakened their sense of a strong ethnic identity.

For many Deaf people, whichever minority ethnic community they belonged to, making alliances across ethnic, religious or hearing–deaf boundaries was not this simple, as noted by a white social services manager:

A lot of people have trouble accepting that Deaf people have their own community, culture, etc., but what happens if you're black or you're Asian and Deaf as well . . . which are you first? You know, are you Asian first and then Deaf or are you Deaf and then Asian, or whatever? And to actually have to deal with two lots of different culture and also have white hearing culture as well in everyday surroundings . . . even Deaf people themselves don't take that on board.

There were variations in the level of awareness about religion and ethnicity among different minority ethnic groups. The Irish Deaf groups within the UK had a strong Catholic emphasis and the Northern Irish and Scottish Deaf Associations were sometimes based around religious groups. Historically the Church Mission Society in the UK provided many of the first Deaf clubs and still trains Chaplains for the Deaf and funds Deaf churches. Members of the Jewish Deaf community were also thought to have acquired a high level of religious awareness through involvement with established Jewish Deaf organizations. In contrast, Asian and African Caribbean Deaf people lacked these resources and were more likely to be engaged in a process of rediscovering their respective religious identities, largely through self-organization. In particular, many felt that young African Caribbean Deaf people had very little relevant provision in this area.

Emergence of social and cultural groups

Since the early 1990s, there has been a growing recognition among service providers as well as minority ethnic Deaf individuals that mainstream services to Deaf people do not take account of cultural and religious needs. There has also been an increased awareness of racist attitudes and practices in the white Deaf community and mainstream services which marginalize minority ethnic Deaf people. Partly as a consequence, a number of social groups have emerged in various parts of the UK which aim to address a variety of user defined needs. Although relatively new among minority ethnic Deaf people, such self-organization among minority ethnic people has a long history (Rex 1991).

These groups varied considerably in terms of their membership, funding sources, lines of accountability and level of user involvement. Some groups consisted of Deaf people who had united on the basis of their 'blackness', while others targeted Deaf people who belonged to a particular ethnic group or had a particular religious affiliation. There were also groups which were exclusively for Deaf Asian women. One group of this nature came into existence as a result of a Deaf Asian woman recognizing that there was no social provision for women like herself. By contacting the youth service and securing some funding from the local community education service, she was able to set up this group. In its five year life, the group had attracted a membership of around 100 Asian Deaf women and was being run successfully by an information and outreach worker with the help of a volunteer, both Deaf Asian women. Not only did they provide information on religious and cultural issues and brought people together to celebrate festivals, such as Diwali, Eid and Christmas, but also they provided health and welfare advice both on an individual basis and through inviting speakers from outside agencies. Women's health was the focus of another African Caribbean Deaf group, which also held sessions on topics such as sexual health and relationships.

Most such groups combined social activities with welfare advice although the range of available activities depended very much on the level of resources available and the specific needs of members attending these groups. Younger members of these groups particularly enjoyed the social and sporting activities and were eager for more outdoor activities to be organized. A hard of hearing group made up of Gujarati elderly men and women valued the information they were provided about environmental aids and adaptations as well as the opportunity to talk about any problems they were having with their hearing aids and text telephones. Members, many not fluent in English, found it helpful to have information in their mother tongue from the Gujarati community development worker who ran the group. Users did not always have the same needs. One profoundly Deafened member of the group complained that his communication needs were being overlooked by the group organizers. Although an English volunteer was available to note-take to aid communication between himself and the group, this was problematic as the volunteer had no knowledge of Gujarati. The Deafened older person expressed his isolation in writing:

> this group hasn't much trouble with hearing . . . they have always loop on their ear. The trouble with this group is that they can't probably understand, speak, write English language, hence they need [Gujarati] interpreter . . . it is actually people like me who are profound deaf needs help to remain in contact through writing. There is nothing for me [here] now.

Having a stronger funding base meant that groups could offer a wider range of social and educational activities and advice. For example, a Jewish Deaf organization, in existence for over 40 years, had a resource centre with a range of special aids and equipment for Deaf people and a day centre for its elderly members. The organization also published a quarterly magazine and provided welfare help.

Joining a Deaf group of this nature provided many Deaf people from minority ethnic communities with a chance to explore their culture and their deafness in an environment in which they felt comfortable. For some it was the only opportunity they had, to be able to relax in the company of other Deaf people, which particularly appealed to those younger Deaf people who were experiencing communication problems with other family members.

The larger social groups also allowed the younger members to meet older Deaf people of the same background, an opportunity they otherwise would not have had. One 17-year-old Pakistani student who regularly attended a women's group always looked forward to meeting older Deaf women: 'I feel that I can learn more from older women because I am a young girl so how will I know what it's like to be an older Asian woman who is married or something? This is the place where I get an opportunity to understand and talk with them.'

Indeed one social group, initially for Deaf Asian adults, was forced to rethink its membership when the organizers were approached by numerous parents of Asian Deaf children asking whether it would be possible for their children to join. Involving young people in groups of this nature was seen as instrumental in developing their ethnic and religious identity, and introducing them to older Deaf role models. The involvement of older Asian Deaf people served to show parents and children the capabilities of Deaf people and work opportunities that were available. According to one Indian woman in her early twenties, one of the reasons why the Deaf women's group she attended had been so successful in empowering, and instilling confidence in, members was that it was run by a Deaf Asian woman whom members regarded as a role model and with whom they could identify: 'to see role models that's very important. I mean, if it's hearing people teaching you all the time it's not gonna work but if you've got a Deaf role model there it's much better.'

The perceived lack of positive role models, noted by both African Caribbean and other respondents, was the reason why a young Deaf African Caribbean student established a Deaf group, which had now been running for two years: 'I want to see black [African Caribbean] people being proud of themselves. At the moment there are very few out there. It would be lovely if people out there could look at other black Deaf people and think I want to be like that.'

Deaf adult role models were thought to be important in presenting positive images for the younger Deaf people. Within the social groups, having minority ethnic Deaf people in positions of power was felt to be important so that they could instill confidence in the younger members and with whom the younger people could identify. Minority ethnic Deaf presenters (especially those working in television) were therefore highly regarded as role models.

Mirroring the debates about accommodating diversity within anti-racism (Modood 1988; Gilroy 1992), there was some concern about separate organization by minority ethnic Deaf people. Some of the young Deaf people felt that ethnically or religiously specific social provision was divisive. Despite recognizing that these social groups had developed in response to the perceived racist marginalization, some still felt that there was a need for unity with other Deaf people facilitated through mixed social groups. A

Deaf African Caribbean student emphasized the shared nature of Deafness which for him united white and black people: 'To tell you the truth I like white and black people to mix. It doesn't matter, we all have eyes and ears and a mouth. We all wear clothes, the only difference is the colour of our skin. It's more friendly if white and black people mix.' However, reflecting the ambivalence felt by many, this respondent went on to comment: 'I hate racism, it just makes things worse.'

Building social networks

There was a widespread keenness among both minority ethnic workers and members of D/deaf social groups to develop links with other social groups of this nature. Many had already visited groups in different parts of Britain; newer groups were particularly eager to learn from the experiences of the more established ones. A number regularly organized parties on religious and social occasions such as Diwali, Eid and Rosh Hashanah. These parties offered the opportunity to get together with other Deaf groups and helped develop a sense of common identity and networks.

Not only were these groups important in terms of bringing Deaf people from minority ethnic communities together, but also some were able to provide a learning environment in which members acquired new skills and interests. The formal courses varied, covering from assertiveness and leadership skills to improving English language skills. Confidence building was regarded as a particularly important issue, as noted by this Asian Deaf professional:

> I really think Asian women are very negative . . . I think they feel like they're not good enough, they want a good education, they want to get a good job but I think they feel, because of the hearing way, you know, you see hearing people and you think, oh very professional, you know, doctors or solicitors, whatever different professions, and I think they feel they just can't do it because they're Deaf and because they're Asian really. I think a lot of the women are like that.

This was far from being universally true, however: in the course of our fieldwork we came across many dynamic and confident Deaf Asian women, some, like this respondent, working in professional jobs.

For one group of young Indian deaf women, the group had allowed them to be informed not only about their ethnicity and traditions but also about Deaf culture. Having had an oral education, they knew little about sign language and the existence of a Deaf community until being exposed to both, through the group. Far from being divisive, their involvement in this social group facilitated greater affinity with the white Deaf people, through an improved knowledge of Deaf culture and politics.

There was considerable variation in the level of involvement that members had in deciding how these groups should be run. In general, members seemed to be consulted on a regular basis about their needs and efforts were made to ensure that these needs could be met. All of these social groups had been encouraged to set up their own management committees. For example, a hearing Asian community development worker had successfully done this with a Deaf Asian group: 'I mean it's very good actually, because before I used to say, "Come on do this", but now they're telling me, "Come on, we want to do this", it's a change.'

There seemed to be a general consensus among members about the aims of these groups and the kinds of activities organized but conflicts did arise. For example, at an Asian Deaf women's group, whose membership included a range of ethnic backgrounds, languages and age groups, at times some of the younger women felt that they were being given information that they already knew about, such as dental health. The needs of younger and older group members often conflicted, as noted by a younger member:

> A lot of Asian Deaf women in the group need to know about information themselves because they never had an education themselves. If they get educated themselves they will know what information they want to look for, whereas with us, we are already educated so we know where to get information, so maybe there needs to be a different group for [younger] people like ourselves.

Tensions also arose because members used the group for different purposes according to personal biographies and needs. While one older married Deaf woman, who had been using the centre for three years, found it very useful to share problems and receive counselling at the group sessions, some younger members preferred to discuss problems with their Deaf friends rather than the counsellors. However, despite expressing these concerns, younger people found the opportunity to be with older Deaf and hearing people of their background beneficial for a variety of other reasons, as discussed earlier.

Identity and cultural sensitivity: some service responses

Respondents felt that mainstream service providers had a large part to play in providing appropriate services. For example, professionals had a responsibility to help the Deaf child become aware of their ethnic and religious background in addition to having a 'Deaf identity'. Educational institutions, health authorities and social services departments were all considered to be major potential catalysts for change in this area, but there was still considerable room for improvement.

Several teachers of Deaf children, based in both schools and colleges for Deaf young people, recognized that their services were not responsive to the needs of students from minority ethnic communities. It was felt that white staff working in such educational institutions needed support and training to learn more about minority ethnic cultures and develop links with families. A Pakistani Deaf student, currently attending a college, was disheartened by the Euro-centric teaching: 'they have no information about our religion or culture. Our culture and religion should be respected equally. There is no information here either for Asian students or for the others.'

This was seen as particularly worrying in residential settings where Deaf students from minority ethnic communities had limited contact with their own ethnic and religious communities and little or no religious input from the staff.

Where schools had taken the initiative to employ someone to teach minority religions, there was a positive response from the children and parents. One Asian hearing man, invited to teach predominantly Muslim children in a school for deaf children about aspects of their religion, recalled how pleased the children were to be able to have this regular contact:

> I was surprised, the kids were really happy, the kids were really happy to see an Asian face in the school. And you know, I really did enjoy it and there were all sorts of questions you know. Varied questions about diet, about food, about dress, 'Are we allowed to wear this? Can we wear that? Can we eat this? Can we eat that? Can we draw pigs? Can we touch pigs?' They can only ask questions at school so how can a Pakistani Asian girl who's 12, 13 ask a white, mid-thirties, early-forties teacher from middle class about her home life? You know, she can't.

Similarly, parental pressure on a service for hearing impaired children precipitated their efforts to set up a cultural awareness class for Deaf Bengali children living in the locality. The weekly classes took place at a secondary school on Saturday mornings and were run by a Bangladeshi tutor with the aid of a sign language interpreter.

The need for specialized services: counselling and interpreting

Many Deaf black people were keen to point out how mainstream services were not addressing their needs, identifying clear gaps in services. Having inadequate access to trained, culturally sensitive, sign language interpreters and counsellors were two of the serious deficiencies highlighted.

Counselling

A number of young Deaf people felt that counselling had a role to play in helping them work through questions of identity. However it was felt that counselling services offered by social services departments were more appropriate for the majority culture and generally not responsive to their needs. White social workers were felt to have little understanding of the pressures and constraints on minority ethnic Deaf people thus making their services relatively inappropriate for minority ethnic users.

Where social workers had been appointed to work with Deaf people, they had found the need to provide some sort of 'cultural counselling' for their younger users. Asian young Deaf people were found to be particularly in need of such counselling. One young Deaf woman was concerned that mainstream service providers did not acknowledge that Deaf people from minority ethnic communities were subject to a range of distressing pressures. She had herself trained as a counsellor and was now working with Deaf minority ethnic individuals and organizations. She talked about her reasons for setting up this specialized service:

> white Deaf people, they have counsellors and they can sort of understand each other but I felt [minority] ethnic groups are different because of their culture and I felt it would need a Deaf Asian person to be able to understand this, to understand the difference in our cultures. I feel we're very, very different and now when I meet people I feel, you know, they find it a lot better to sort of express themselves because they see me as a good role model.

Sign language interpreting

It was widely acknowledged that there was a shortage of BSL interpreters who were from minority ethnic communities and fluent in their mother tongue. Nine sign language interpreters, the majority African Caribbean, were identified as working either in a freelance capacity or employed by organizations working with Deaf people. A recently formed organization 'Black and Asian Sign Language Interpreters' has set out to redress this shortfall in numbers and the quality of appropriate interpreting. There was an expectation that such interpreters would better understand the experiences of and problems confronting minority ethnic Deaf people. One African Caribbean interpreter recalled an occasion when she interpreted for a group of Deaf Asian women. She found their positive response pleasing considering that she was of a different ethnic background. She feels that what mattered to the women was that she showed an appreciation and understanding of their background and culture. Another African Caribbean interpreter talked about the rapport she could develop while working with black Deaf people: 'You walk into a room, a black Deaf person sees you and their face lights up, and it's like, yes, and there's an automatic link that you have. It doesn't breach impartiality but it's there.'

Having worked with Deaf minority ethnic people for several years, this interpreter was in no doubt that it was better to use interpreters from minority ethnic backgrounds to work with minority ethnic Deaf people. Another African Caribbean interpreter commented:

> I've observed someone [white] interpreting for a black client who [the client] was very restricted in her signing. When I took over, she suddenly seemed to let loose and express herself much more . . . later she said to me 'Usually [white] people think I'm really angry but I'm not

angry'. I thought to myself that she was not doing anything to indicate that she was angry. I have seen interpreters assume they [black people] are angry. It's like with hearing people when they [Deaf people] get excited [hearing] people think 'they're going to hit me'.

Politicization as well as empathy and cultural understanding were issues addressed by others. An African Caribbean interpreter spoke of her own politicization as well as that of the Deaf people with whom she worked:

In the early days, I never thought about what colour I was, whether I were pink, green or blue. Then I noticed that whenever I turned up to interpret for black or Asian people they always looked really pleased to see me. As I became more aware myself, I realized that it was pride, really that's the only way that I can describe it. I was sort of like a role model . . . a black role model.

Signs and cultural signifiers for African Caribbean or Asian people and cultures were not always picked up by white interpreters. Differences in the use of sign language between ethnic, social and age groups have been noted by others (see Ahmad *et al.* 1998: ch. 3). The interpreter referred to above, gave the example of 'hot combs' used in the 1970s to straighten hair, which needed a new sign. She also commented that the use of the hot comb sometimes left burn marks on the neck and 'Deaf people notice that kind of thing'. Black Deaf people did not like constantly being asked about the burn marks by white Deaf people. This interpreter, as an African Caribbean woman, felt a strong sense of support too from Asian Deaf women when working with them; she felt that this was because she had taken the trouble to acquire basic information about Asian communities, for example knowing signs for food (such as samosas and chapattis) and distinctions between different Asian groups (such as Pakistanis or Indians). As an interpreter working with minority ethnic Deaf young people, she felt that 'racism both individual and institutional' made it harder for them and their parents to learn about available support.

African Caribbean and Asian people were grossly under-represented in the area of sign language interpreting and little was being done to increase their numbers among trainee interpreters. For example, a trainee interpreter of Indian origin, based at a Deaf Centre serving a multi-ethnic Deaf population, felt that more people from minority ethnic communities were needed to train as BSL interpreters. She felt that little was being done to promote the services of sign language interpreters with competency in minority ethnic languages and she, like the African Caribbean interpreter above, felt that having access to an interpreter of the same ethnic background made a real difference. Consequently African Caribbean or Asian interpreters were a much sought-after commodity:

I went on a course recently and somebody was Deaf there and said, 'Oh I didn't know there were any Asian interpreters in the country and oh, wow, wow, wow, I'll pass your name around,' sort of thing and somebody else had heard recently, was a friend of mine who went to do some work and was asked did she know of any Asian interpreters because they wanted to set up provisions for Deaf [people].

It was also felt that the inappropriate use of signs to describe aspects of non-white cultures reflected the racism in the white Deaf world. Some of the signs which were previously used for a number of African and Asian countries, people or customs were considered to be derogatory. Some are being replaced with more appropriate signs and new signs are being developed to describe aspects of ethnic minority cultures, food and dress.

A number of African Caribbean sign language interpreters highlighted the fact that African Caribbean Deaf people were prevented from learning about their own heritage without realizing it, all because no signs existed to explain behaviour and practices pertaining to their own culture. This was regarded as less of a problem for Asian people whose 'cultural distinctiveness' was generally accepted within Deaf culture (Ahmad *et al.* 1998). Similarly Jewish Deaf people could not understand why no commonly understood signs existed for their festivals or customs.

Discussion

The evidence in this chapter paints a mixed picture. At a positive level, there is much welcome activity on a range of issues of concern to minority ethnic D/deaf people and their families. The fact that many of these initiatives are relatively new indicates both a recent recognition by service providers and assertiveness and organization on the part of minority ethnic Deaf people and their families. However, worryingly, the evidence also shows continued problems of short-termism, relative lack of mainstream activity and initiatives being driven by committed individuals in services without their ownership by the organization. Evidence for any major shift, either in the mainstream Deaf culture or services for Deaf people, is thin. The perennial problems of funding and organizing services for minority ethnic communities, both Deaf and hearing, are discussed elsewhere (Ahmad *et al.* 1998). Here we discuss issues concerning identity politics, self-help and services.

Identity and organization

An interesting aspect of what we have reported is that much of the user-led activity so strongly revolves around ethnicity, culture and religion; in some ways a quest for a rediscovery of forms of identity which are crucial to people's lives. These forms of identity were often denied to Deaf people for a variety of reasons. First, education in schools has little focus on minority religions, languages and cultures (Chamba *et al.* 1998a), something pointed out by many young people, their parents and teachers. The Euro-centricity of educational provision was resented by many and is powerfully illustrated in the words of the mother who remarks: 'I send my child to school and he comes back an Englishman'. Second, Deaf culture remains predominantly white and Christian. Although religious and cultural diversity in Deaf culture is beginning to be recognized, Deaf culture is not yet able to fully accommodate or service this diversity. Third, parents and families have often not been able to communicate easily with their Deaf children and hence Deaf people have had less exposure to their own ethnic culture than would be normal for a hearing person. Many of these issues are addressed in Ahmad *et al.* (1998) and Chamba *et al.* (1998a). However, the developments must not be seen only in negative terms; rediscovery and reaffirmation of different forms of identity is not unique to minority ethnic Deaf people. Identity is a potent means of social organization and of giving meaning to personal and group level beliefs, aspirations and behaviour (see Joly 1987; Rex 1991; on religious mobilization, see Samad 1992).

That personal identities are negotiated, flexible and situational is also evident in many of the initiatives discussed here. Social and cultural activity was organized on a variety of grounds: gender, with both young and older people; religion; ethnicity, broadly defined in terms of say 'Asian', though local residence patterns often meant that most users had a shared cultural, linguistic and religious background; and Deaf identity. The organization at these different levels clearly had advantages and disadvantages. For example, the young Deaf women, who were joined by older hearing women, while resenting the fact that much of what was discussed around Deafness was already known to them, were appreciative of the fact that the older women allowed them to know what was expected of themselves as they grow older. For the younger Deaf women, these older women were a major source of cultural knowledge and normative assumptions about behaviour. Yet in other cases, groups emphasized the shared nature of Deafness as being their primary identifier. Ethnicity, religion and other cultural identities were secondary, their assertion being regarded as divisive. The negotiated nature of identity is discussed by Drury (1991), Modood *et al.* (1994) and Ahmad (1996).

Empowerment and professionalization

One strong feature in the Deaf movement since the 1980s is the emergence of Deaf professionals and the proliferation of educational and vocational courses aimed at Deaf people. This was also an issue addressed in some of the initiatives. The importance of role models was emphasized by many. In particular, the relative shortage of African Caribbean role models was noted by respondents as was their relative lack of organization compared to Asian Deaf people. Through the fieldwork and personal contacts, we have noted an increase in minority ethnic Deaf professionals, most themselves working with Deaf people. The increased self-organization and improved formal recognition of diversity among Deaf people should improve training and education opportunities for minority ethnic Deaf people in years to come.

The impact of organization around social and cultural issues may also have positive outcomes in terms of personal development. Broadly, we note four areas of impact relevant to personal development. First, such groups provided opportunities for networking and discovering positive role models, both Deaf and hearing. The importance of role models is well recognized in literature on educational achievement and ethnicity (Cashmore and Troyna 1990). Second, they offered access to information and resources. This was important both to families of Deaf people who, according to some respondents, often had low expectations for their Deaf family members, and to Deaf people themselves. Access to information remains a problem for large sections of the minority ethnic population (see Atkin and Rollings 1993); for Deaf people this is an even bigger problem (Ahmad *et al.* 1998; Chamba *et al.* 1998a, 1998b). Third, a positive identity, which many seemed to be acquiring through their involvement in the range of social activities, is in itself an important element of self-development. Finally, the groups offered an important source of social support, which many felt was absent from white Deaf culture. As we have noted, although the white Deaf culture is increasingly acknowledging diversity among Deaf people, there is much room for progress, and many still experience racist marginalization within the Deaf culture.

Sign language interpreting

It was generally acknowledged that there was a shortage of minority ethnic sign language interpreters, particularly an acute shortage of Asian interpreters. The need will be met only by improved recruitment of people from the relevant minority ethnic communities. The advantages of having more interpreters from Asian and other minority ethnic groups are several and varied. The most obvious one is that there is a dearth of interpreters who can work between BSL and languages other than English. Second, white interpreters often do not have the requisite knowledge of minority ethnic customs, rituals, foods and festivals – examples of this are given in interviews with African Caribbean interpreters. Many also pointed out the racism of British Sign Language, although many of the openly offensive signs are being changed. Third, some felt that even where both interpreters and Deaf people from minority ethnic communities did not share a common culture or language, they had shared experiences of minority status within a dominant white culture, which improved rapport and encouraged trust. The lack of training opportunities and the failure to attract minority ethnic trainee interpreters, however, remains a problem to be urgently addressed.

Forgotten minorities

Much of the activity remains confined to Asian and African Caribbean Deaf people who use BSL. Very few initiatives aimed at the Chinese or other smaller or dispersed communities were identified. Further, the limited activity focusing on smaller communities that we identified is concentrated largely in London where there are some services which are targeted at refugees and other groups. There must be an unmet need for support among Deaf people from these many and varied communities supported by the stratagem of small numbers or that 'they look after their own' (see Walker and Ahmad 1994 for more general discussion). Both service providers and the wider Deaf community must take action to end this marginalization.

Finally, we find little support for the common stereotype, of Asian parents' supposed passivity or fatalism. Parents and families took advantage of opportunities to improve their knowledge and skills, encouraged their Deaf children to engage in activities that they felt were beneficial, and supported each other through networking and information exchange.

Conclusion

After decades of neglect, the existence of minority ethnic D/deaf people is beginning to be acknowledged by service organizations. However, much innovative self-organization by minority ethnic Deaf people centres around issues of identity where alongside the ownership of a Deaf identity, other identity claims relating to religion and culture are being cultivated and sustained. On the whole this shows a positive assertion of, often neglected aspects of minority ethnic Deaf people's self-hood. However, behind this self-organization is also the realization that the broader Deaf culture is Euro-centric and at times racist. Self-organization around identity confirms both the commonality of their experience as Deaf people as well as pride in and a celebration of other identity claims.

Acknowledgements

We thank the Joseph Rowntree Foundation for generously supporting this work, Gohar Nisar for help with fieldwork, the many respondents for their time and the Advisory Committee for their guidance.

Note

1 We follow the convention of referring to people who define themselves as culturally deaf and part of the deaf community, and who use British Sign Language as a first language, as 'Deaf' with an upper case 'D'. People with acquired deafness often do not regard themselves as part of the 'Deaf community' and are referred to as 'deaf' with a lower case 'd'. In case of overlap D/deaf is used.

6

Language, communication and information: the needs of parents caring for a severely disabled child

Rampaul Chamba and Waqar I.U. Ahmad

Parents need to be informed of the disability as soon as possible so they can be given support they need to cope. In my daughter's case, I was not told anything at all, although the doctors knew straight away. I found out after a few months when my daughter started to have fits.

I need a lot of questions answered regarding his medical condition but who do I question or where do I get information. Social services are no help to parents who can't speak English. They think you are capable of filling the forms yourself.

I have experienced so many difficulties with my house as it was not safe for [child's name]. We were given a grant to have it repaired but the work is all still there and this is only because we cannot speak good English. When my husband filled the forms for the grant he said to have the roof and windows repaired . . . but because we did not fill the forms correctly, that work is still there. Now we have to pay twice as much to have it repaired.

These direct quotations from parents indicate the hardships caused by barriers to communication based in the inability of services to respond to the needs of non-speakers of English. However, as this chapter makes clear, communication is more than the sum of matched languages or provision of interpreters. It is a process in which language, cultural background and knowledge, social class, information about the workings of the welfare system and a match between the information provided and the perceived needs of users, all play an important part. The chapter is based on the findings of the first major survey of minority ethnic parents of severely disabled children to have been conducted in Britain (Chamba *et al.* 1999); Chapters 7 and 8 also focus on the relationship between users and services.

Language structures thought and identities and mediates social interaction. It is the vehicle through which meaning is negotiated and communication takes place. However, more than just a tool for communication, language is interwoven with cultural, religious and moral proprieties and furnishes the character given to identities, perspectives, cultural forms and ethnic groups. Diverse languages contribute to multiculturalism and poly-ethnic societies. And language and communication have particular importance in social policy. Many people from minority ethnic groups may not share the language of the majority population. This may impact on their ability to access welfare services and thus be denied a basic element of substantive citizenship (Andrews 1991; Ahmad and Husband 1993).

Over the years, health, education and social care policy and legislation have attempted to reflect the demographic constitution of society and differences in language, culture and religion in order to make services more appropriate and accessible. In practice, this has usually been done through the provision of interpreters and information in appropriate languages. Policy and legislation gives structural legitimacy to formal citizenship and the management of diversity within a poly-ethnic society. Welfare services are meant to enact and facilitate the realization of these citizenship rights through the appropriate allocation of resources and professional services. The needs of minority ethnic users, however, are often marginalized through racist exclusion, convenient dictums of 'they care for their own', and the unwillingness of services to cater equitably for the needs of non-speakers of English.

Use and command of English – level of ability to speak, read and write English – do vary considerably between ethnic groups (Office for National Statistics (ONS) 1996; Modood *et al.* 1997). Despite the diversity of languages used, spoken English is usually the chief means of communication with professionals. The ability to read and write English is also important in learning about services. Parents' inability to communicate effectively in English is likely to impinge on their experience of caring for a disabled child in a number of ways. It affects their attempts to reduce the impact of poor living circumstances by, for example, ensuring the receipt of benefits and resolution of housing problems. It may impede communication with professionals and entail a reliance on professional interpreters or, more commonly, on family and friends. It may also reduce the amount of accessible information. Previous research shows that minority ethnic carers are more disadvantaged in access to services and remain poorly informed about services and entitlements (Yee 1995). Considering that white English-speaking parents caring for a severely disabled child report problems in communication with professionals and a lack of adequate information (Baldwin and Carlisle 1994; Beresford 1995), hurdles faced by non-users of English would be considerably greater even if we neglect barriers related to racism or unwarranted assumptions on the part of professionals about less need for support among minority ethnic groups (see Ahmad and Husband 1993).

Evidence of greater disadvantage faced by minority ethnic carers of disabled people continues to mount, albeit based on relatively small-scale studies (see review by Atkin and Rollings 1993; see also Chapters 2, 7 and 8 in this volume).

In light of the particular importance of communication, this chapter describes the findings of a major national survey of minority ethnic parents caring for a severely disabled child. The questions raised in that survey extended to those about income, housing and benefits, contact with professionals, support groups and unmet need (Chamba *et al.* 1999). Questions about language, communication and information were vital to parental experiences; we focus first on the languages that parents used including their ability to speak, read and write English. Second, parents' reported need for and provision of interpreters, both professional and lay, and their experiences are described. Third, we look at parents' views on the information they received about their child's impairment and sources of help, followed by their preferences for the way in which information could be provided. We conclude by discussing some of the implications of lack of information and difficulties in communication in the context of the varied demands experienced by minority ethnic parents caring for a severely disabled child.

The study

The sample

This study replicated an earlier survey of mainly white parents of severely disabled children (Beresford 1995); to aid comparison, it followed the research design used by Beresford. The sample for the survey was drawn from the Family Fund Trust (FFT) database of families with a severely disabled child.[1] The FFT database began collecting data on the ethnic origin and first language of all new applicants in April 1996. Two techniques were employed for obtaining the desired sample. First, names generated from the FFT ethnic monitoring data were supplemented by name analysis and assigning these to different languages and religions for Asian families using a software package called *Nam Pehchan* (Identifying Names).[2] Second, additional Black Caribbean and Black African families were identified through consultation with FFT Visitors.[3]

Three main criteria were used for including families within the sample, which was stratified by age group and gender: only children under the age of 15 years were included; only very severely disabled children were included, that is those whose applications passed the FFT's stringent eligibility criteria; and to avoid overburdening families with demands of research, only families who had not previously participated in research through the FFT were included. A total of 1072 families were identified to approach. The approximated language groups to which parents were assigned is shown in Table 6.1.

Table 6.1 Language group of questionnaires

Assumed language group	No.
Urdu	327
Punjabi	238
Gujarati	181
Bengali	106
Hindi	25
English (Black African/Caribbean)	195
Base	1072

The questionnaire

To aid comparison, the overall structure and content of the questionnaire were retained from Beresford's (1995) study. However, to ensure cultural appropriateness of the questionnaire and to cover issues of language and communication, modifications and additions were made following consultations with parents of disabled children and professionals with experience in this area. The final questionnaire was translated into five Asian languages – Urdu, Punjabi, Gujarati, Bengali and Hindi – for the Asian families within the sample. Translations were validated through independent assessors. Apart from using largely fixed response categories to ease completion, parents were also asked to note additional comments pertinent to their experiences; this chapter begins with some of these open-ended responses.

The parent with main caring responsibility and contact with services was requested to complete the questionnaire. An additional form, translated for Asian parents, allowed parents to request a questionnaire in a different language and/or to request help with filling in the questionnaire. Assistance with completing the questionnaire was offered by conducting a telephone interview or arranging for a home visit by a FFT Visitor or other appropriate person.

Response rate

A total of 647 completed questionnaires were returned, a response rate of 60 per cent. After excluding 60 respondents because they failed some aspect of our inclusion criteria, 587 were included in the final analysis.

The parents

The vast majority of respondents were mothers (86 per cent), not surprising in that the questionnaire was to be completed by the main carers. Questions on ethnicity in the questionnaire allowed parents to be allocated to appropriate ethnic groups. The number of respondents in the Indian, Pakistani and Black Caribbean groups were adequate for analysis. The Black African

Table 6.2   Religion by ethnicity (%)

Religion	Black African/ Caribbean	Indian	Pakistani	Bangladeshi
Judaeo-Christian	86	1	—	—
Sikh	—	56	—	—
Hindu	—	29	—	—
Muslim	14	14	100	100
Base (= 100%)	108	211	154	70

group was too small on its own and was merged with the Black Caribbean group to form the Black African/Caribbean group. With the exception of combining Black Africans with Black Caribbeans, the ethnic categories used replicate those employed in the 1991 Census.

Parents were also asked to state their religion in an open-ended question and their responses were classified into four main religious groups. Table 6.2 describes parents' religion by ethnicity.

Three-quarters of parents were married or living as married. Over half of Black African/Caribbean parents were single compared with fewer than 2 per cent of Asian parents. Parents' ages ranged from 18 to just over 60; the average age was 35 years. There was little variation in ages between ethnic groups. Family size ranged from those with only the disabled child to one family with twelve children. Caring for a disabled child can be more difficult if the parent has a disability or suffers from poor health, and demands of caring can, in turn, exacerbate parents' ill-health. Almost one-quarter of parents described their health as poor or very poor (see also Chapters 2 and 8).

The disabled children

All parents were caring for a severely disabled child. Children with a range of physical impairments and/or learning difficulties and those with chronic or other life threatening illnesses were represented. All children were under 15 years of age. Indian and Bangladeshi children were somewhat older than Black African/Caribbean and Pakistani children. Just over half (54 per cent) of the respondents were parents of boys (n = 317) and 46 per cent were parents of girls (n = 270). Overall, stratification of this sample by age and gender was similar to Beresford's (1995) study. Chamba *et al.* (1999) provide detailed findings from this survey, including comparisons with Beresford's study.

Language use and diversity

Variations in the use and command of English warrants professional and institutional attention to ensure that non-users of English are not disadvant-aged. Table 6.3 shows, as expected, that more Black African/Caribbean

Table 6.3 Use of English by ethnicity (%)

Use of English	Black African/ Caribbean	Indian	Pakistani	Bangladeshi
Speaking	96	81	68	47
Reading	84	72	54	42
Writing	82	71	52	35
Base (= 100%)	133	214	155	71

parents used English than any other group of parents. Moreover, there is a clear gradient across the Asian groups, with English being more widely used by Indian parents than by Pakistani and Bangladeshi parents. In each ethnic group, more parents could speak English than read or write it. Fewer than half the Bangladeshi parents could speak English. As discussed later in this chapter, this was consistent with their greater need for an interpreter when talking to professionals.

The ability to use the English language does not mean that it is the first language of choice within ethnic minority communities. The backgrounds of Asian populations reflect different languages, dialects, cultures and geographical areas. The survey findings mirrored this linguistic diversity. Table 6.4 shows that while Hindi, Gujarati and Bengali were associated with particular ethnic groups, the use of Punjabi and Urdu extended across Indian and Pakistani parents. The findings also indicate that 29 per cent of Indian parents and 43 per cent of Pakistani parents spoke two or more of the languages represented here. As with the use of English, the ability to speak a language was more widespread than to read and write. The particularly steep gradient between fluency and literacy in Punjabi for the Pakistani population shows that most Punjabi speakers from Pakistan use Urdu as the written language.

Understanding spoken English

Spoken English is likely to be the chief means of communication with professionals despite the diversity of languages used by parents. Parents of disabled children generally complain of not having adequate information about their child's condition, services available for the child, and support available for parents (see Baldwin and Carlisle 1994; Beresford 1995). Parents with little use of English may well be even more disadvantaged (Atkin and Rollings 1996). Although a majority of parents said that they could use the English language, not all of them felt that they could communicate adequately. Overall, 63 per cent (356 parents) reported that they had complete understanding of spoken English; 23 per cent (131) some understanding; 12 per cent (69) a little understanding; and 3 per cent (14) no understanding at all. More than one-third of all parents therefore felt that they had a less than full understanding of spoken English.

Table 6.4 Languages used by Asian parents (%)

Asian language	Indian	Pakistani	Bangladeshi
Punjabi			
Speaking	55	63	—
Reading	26	9	—
Writing	24	6	—
Urdu			
Speaking	11	68	—
Reading	2	52	—
Writing	1	44	—
Hindi			
Speaking	28	3	3
Reading	14	—	—
Writing	12	—	—
Gujarati			
Speaking	35	—	—
Reading	24	—	—
Writing	22	—	—
Bengali			
Speaking	1	1	82
Reading	—	1	50
Writing	—	1	50
Base	220	161	72

Parents' ability to understand spoken English varied by ethnicity (see Table 6.5). As might be expected, more Black African/Caribbean parents said that they had complete understanding of spoken English than any of the Asian groups. Among the latter, two-thirds of Indian parents and half of Pakistani parents said they understood spoken English completely but only one-quarter of Bangladeshi parents did so. Bangladeshi parents were most disadvantaged, with almost half reporting little or no understanding of spoken English. The variation between ethnic groups was greater than would be expected by chance (that is, it was statistically significant).

These variations by ethnicity in parents' ability to speak English were reflected across the religious communities, with Muslims being more disadvantaged than Hindus. Within the Muslim group, however, more Indian and Pakistani Muslims understood English well (57 and 54 per cent respectively) than did Bangladeshi Muslim parents (26 per cent).

Parents' need for an interpreter

Services for disabled children rarely employ bilingual workers; in some areas having some bilingual workers would not be sufficient to cater for the

Table 6.5 Understanding spoken English by ethnicity (%)

Spoken English	Black African/ Caribbean	Indian	Pakistani	Bangladeshi
Complete understanding	89	64	53	29
Some understanding	8	30	25	26
Little understanding	2	6	21	30
No understanding	1	1	1	16
Base (= 100%)	132	213	155	70

Note: Chi-square = 151.0, df = 9, p < 0.001

diversity of linguistic needs in the user population. Further, effective communication requires not only a knowledge of language but also the cultural and service context in which communication takes place. Thus, at times, even fairly competent users of English may well need an interpreter. Overall, 34 per cent of Asian parents (145) felt that they needed an interpreter when talking to professionals but of these, no more than six out of ten (85 parents) said they were actually provided with one. Otherwise they relied on a family member or friend to interpret for them.

Expressed need for, and provision of, an interpreter largely reflected parents' reported ability to understand spoken English. Thus, the proportion of parents who said that they would need an interpreter when talking to professionals ranged from 61 per cent of those with some understanding of spoken English, through 84 per cent of those with a little understanding, to 92 per cent of those with no understanding. The proportion of parents who said that they were usually provided with an interpreter also increased as the ability to understand spoken English declined (from 39 per cent through 49 per cent, and 62 per cent, respectively). Fewer than 4 per cent of parents with complete understanding said that they needed or were provided with interpreters. That some parents who reported to have a complete understanding of English felt the need to use an interpreter may relate to their concerns about lacking sufficient grasp of service context or technical jargon.

Consistent with Bangladeshi parents having limited understanding of English, Table 6.6 shows that they were more likely to express a need for interpreters than Indian and Pakistani parents (60 per cent compared with 22 per cent and 38 per cent, respectively), a difference greater than would be expected to have occurred by chance. Perhaps reflecting different approaches to interpreter provision between areas in which different ethnic groups reside, Bangladeshi parents were more likely to be provided with an interpreter (46 per cent compared with 12 per cent and 23 per cent, respectively for Indian and Pakistani parents). Table 6.6 shows that 72 per cent of the Bangladeshi parents needing an interpreter were usually provided with one, compared with 60 per cent of Pakistani and 50 per cent of Indian parents. However, these findings do not mean that Indian parents are more

Table 6.6   Need for and provision of interpreters by ethnicity (%)

Interpreters	Indian	Pakistani	Bangladeshi
Need for an interpreter[a]	22	38	60
Provision of interpreters[b]	12	23	46
Base	206	153	67

Notes:
a Chi-square = 35.5, df = 2, p < 0.001
b Chi-square = 36.8, df = 2, p < 0.001

likely to have an unmet need for interpreters. This conclusion is unjustified without knowing parents' preferences for interpreting support and the alternatives available to them.

Parents' experience of using interpreters provided by professionals
Professional interpreting requires a range of skills, reflective of often dealing with complex information in two languages where direct equivalence of terms may not be available. Also, to aid communication between the two parties, the interpreter needs to know the service context, have some knowledge of the child's condition and its implications, and be sensitive to both parental and professional goals for particular encounters. That interpreting rarely meets these ideals is reported by others (Chamba *et al.* 1998b; see also Atkin *et al.*, Chapter 7 in this volume). Chamba *et al.* (1998b) also note that professionals rarely have any training in work with interpreters. Parents were asked about the advantages and disadvantages of using professional interpreters by presenting them with eleven statements describing how helpful or otherwise such support had been. Overall, 153 parents agreed with at least one of the statements, 84 per cent of those who needed an interpreter when talking to professionals.

Almost half of the parents valued the opportunity to use interpreters because they allowed them to 'say what I want', something denied to many parents who were managing without an interpreter or with inadequate interpreting support (Table 6.7). One in three parents valued not having to rely on friends or relatives for interpreting, while 15 per cent appreciated the confidentiality that an independent interpreter can offer. However, there was widespread dissatisfaction with the interpreters provided by professionals and almost all parents maintained that such support was inadequate in some way or that interpreting support was not always readily available. Almost one-quarter of parents reported that the interpreters did not know enough about the child's disability, but there were also difficulties with the quality of interpreting (inaccuracies or use of difficult words), as well as insensitivity to parents' particular needs and circumstances (lack of confidentiality or an unsympathetic approach).

Table 6.7 Experience of using professional interpreters by ethnicity (%)

Experience of using interpreters	Indian	Pakistani	Bangladeshi
Gives me a chance to say what I want	31	52	65
Do not have to rely on family or friends	38	37	29
Provides confidentiality from family and friends	16	19	12
No interpreting available	27	23	24
Interpreters know little or nothing about disability	27	14	21
Interpreting is not confidential	24	14	12
Takes too long to get an interpreter	16	15	15
Interpreting is not accurate	13	11	15
Interpreters do not speak my dialect	7	19	9
Interpreters use difficult words	22	6	—
Interpreting not done in a sympathetic way	4	5	3
Other experiences of using interpreters	11	8	12
Base (= 100%)	45	65	34

Note: Percentages sum to more than 100 because of multiple response

Consistent with variations across ethnic groups in their understanding and use of spoken English, Bangladeshi parents most valued the opportunity that interpreters provided to say what they wanted and Indian parents found an interpreter least useful. Otherwise, differences between the ethnic groups were not large. Difficulties in obtaining an interpreter, for example, were commonly experienced by all groups. However, Pakistani parents were more likely to experience frustration in finding an interpreter who knew their particular dialect while more Indian parents were concerned about understanding the words used by interpreters. Both Indian and Bangladeshi parents were more likely to report that interpreters have little understanding of their child's disability. Overall, Indian parents were most likely to report negative experiences of using professional interpreters which may reflect higher expectations of service providers on their part (see Table 6.7). These findings are consistent with those reported from qualitative studies (Chamba *et al.* 1998b; see also Chapter 7), suggesting that technical competence is an insufficient criterion for judging interpreting. Accessibility of language, knowledge of the service context, confidentiality and an empathetic approach are all important; and that professionals also need skills in working with interpreters.

Using lay interpreters
In addition to professional interpreters, many parents reported that a family member or friend would act as an interpreter. Overall, one in four of all parents (157) said that they would ask a friend or relative to act as an interpreter. Of those who appreciated that a professional interpreter meant that they did not have to rely on family or friends or that it offered greater

Table 6.8 Unmet needs for information by ethnicity (%)

Information need	Black African/ Caribbean	Indian	Pakistani	Bangladeshi
Child's impairment[a]	57	29	34	18
Services for disabled child[b]	75	59	63	39
Support for parents[c]	75	62	69	43
Base	130	210	153	65

Notes:
a Chi-square = 38.7, df = 3, p < 0.01
b Chi-square = 25.1, df = 3, p < 0.01
c Chi-square = 21.5, df = 3, p < 0.01

confidentiality, one-half said that they also used a friend or relative. Among these families, spouses or partners, other family members and children were most likely to act as interpreters. Many parents relied on two or three individuals from their immediate and wider family at different times to act as interpreters. Compared with Indian and Pakistani parents, Bangladeshi parents were somewhat more likely to ask their children, rather than their partner, to interpret for them. This is consistent with fewer Bangladeshi parents having a good command of spoken English but, overall, the use of family and friends as interpreters varied little across ethnic groups.

Parents were also asked who *usually* acted as their interpreter. Altogether, of 130 parents, the vast majority mentioned that a social worker (88 per cent) and/or their children (84 per cent) usually helped with interpreting. In addition, 65 per cent mentioned their spouse or partner, 56 per cent used friends of the family and 45 per cent were helped by relatives other than their immediate family. Differences between ethnic groups were small.

Information

Information about the child's condition and services is an important re-source which helps parents cope with the demands of caring for a disabled child and plan for the future. Parents, however, often cope with inadequate information about their child's impairment, services and support available for their disabled child, and for themselves (Ward 1990; Beresford 1995; Beresford *et al.* 1996). Parents' information needs can be especially neg-lected if they do not speak English, and where services are insensitive to different cultural norms and expectations. Variations in use and command of English, need for and provision of interpreters and reliance on family and friends for interpreting support are likely to shape parents' ability to access sufficient, appropriate and timely information.

Parents were asked whether they had enough information about their child's impairment, the services and support for their disabled child, and for themselves (Table 6.8). Overall, 70 per cent of parents said that they did not have enough information in one or more of these areas, especially on sources of support for the child and themselves. Unmet needs for information about support services, whether for their disabled child or themselves, were twice as likely to be mentioned than lack of information about their child's impairment. The pattern of unmet needs was similar across ethnic groups. Each group had a greater unmet need for information about services and support than they did about their child's disability. Black African/Caribbean parents were more likely to report unmet needs for information than Asian families. Among the latter group, Bangladeshi parents were least likely to feel that they had unmet needs in the three areas of information but this may reflect their lower expectations of service providers as sources of information.

The findings summarized in Table 6.8 appear to be inconsistent with variations in the use of and command over English described above (Tables 6.3 and 6.5). Considering their greater command of English, Black African/Caribbean parents would be expected to have fewer unmet needs for information than Asian parents, especially Pakistani and Bangladeshi parents who have least understanding of spoken and written English. The similar pattern of responses from Pakistani and Indian parents and the differences between Pakistani and Bangladeshi parents also do not reflect variations in parents' ability to use English language. These differences are also inconsistent with the finding that, on the whole, parents who said that they had enough information about their child's disability, information about services and support for themselves consistently reported fewer housing problems than parents who did not. Bangladeshi parents on the whole reported most housing problems, yet they also report fewer unmet needs for information.

These inconsistencies suggest that while command of English is related to unmet needs for information, there may be a much more pervasive gap in the availability of information for all groups accounting for high levels of unmet need among Black African/Caribbean parents. While the ability to speak and understand English was important, other factors, such as attending support groups and the nature of parents' relationship with professionals, were also important for parents as ways of acquiring information. Furthermore, questions about satisfaction are notoriously difficult to interpret. Responses are influenced by knowledge, previous experience and expectations. It is likely that those with low expectations would be more satisfied with services irrespective of quality. An example of this is a study which showed that although Bangladeshi mothers using child health services received relatively poor services compared to white mothers, they were more satisfied with services (Watson 1984). Findings based on self-reported perceptions of need and satisfaction thus need to be interpreted with caution.

How parents would like more information

Information can be provided in a variety of forms but services have, on the whole, continued to rely on written translations. More innovative ways of

Table 6.9 How parents would like more information by ethnicity (%)

Source of information	Black African/ Caribbean	Indian	Pakistani	Bangladeshi
A named worker	51	42	52	51
Written information (e.g. leaflets)	51	48	48	31
Videos on child's disability	57	34	32	36
Professionals	26	43	32	34
Advice centre	39	41	23	33
Videos on services	41	34	28	33
Other parent/support groups	41	29	19	13
Telephone help-line in English	20	22	14	10
Telephone help-line in other languages	3	16	19	21
Other	4	6	6	—
Base (= 100%)	124	193	145	61

Note: Percentages sum to more than 100 because of multiple response

disseminating information such as videos have also emerged (Jones and Pullen 1995). Parents' preferences of how they would like to receive information, however, suggest that no one particular source of information was dominant. On average, each family mentioned three possibilities which suggests that they would be receptive to being informed in a variety of ways. Almost half the parents would welcome more information from a named person or key worker and/or in written form. Over one-third of parents suggested information in video form directly from professional workers, or from advice centres. Fewer than three out of ten parents thought that parent support groups would be helpful (see discussion of support groups in Chamba *et al.* 1999). Telephone help-lines, whether in English or another language, were not widely seen as a way of getting information. This would suggest that the association between use and command of English and information needs is more complex and not guided solely by language difficulties as discussed in more detail below. Table 6.9 gives details of parental preferences for sources of information.

Language, communication and information as resources for caring

The effect of poor use and command of English on caring for a disabled child is not circumscribed to limited episodes as all contact with professionals and services is mediated by communication. It exerts a long-term effect on the whole trajectory of caring for a disabled child. Since all contacts with professionals, services and forms of support are negotiated, mainly through English, the consequences of poor use and command of English are not marginal to the experience of caring, acquisition of information and importance of having collaborative relationships with professionals (Chamba *et al.* 1999). Thus, use and command of English impinged on parents' abilities to draw on a range of resources for helping them cope with caring.

Comparably fewer minority ethnic parents than the mainly white parents in Beresford's (1995) study received benefits. Those who received benefits were given these at lower rates than parents in Beresford's (1995) survey. Asian parents were missing out on benefits and information to which they may be entitled due to limited understanding of English. It also affected parents' ability to negotiate other aspects of living circumstances such as filling in application forms related to adapting their home. Large numbers of parents expressed concern about not knowing what services were available, not knowing where to go for information, having difficulty in making themselves understood, not always understanding what they were told, or feeling that the information was insensitive to their culture or religion. Others show that information given in the abstract gains real value only when a concrete situation for its application arises (see Chapter 7). For example, Atkin *et al.* (Chapter 7) note parents' experiences of coping with the first painful crisis experienced by their children with sickle cell disorder. The value of information given in the abstract became recognized only when applied to the real experience of dealing with the child's pain. Atkin *et al.* (Chapter 7) note that parents required information which allowed them to cope with adversity when it was faced; this required the flexibility to test out their understandings and to seek additional information as the need arose. Such flexibility is not always available to parents of disabled children.

Collaborative relationships with professionals as opposed to those marked by mutual disrespect and antagonism were more likely to be underpinned by effective communication, understanding and exchange of information whether this is done using an interpreter or not. Thus, parents reported fewer unmet needs when they described their relationship with professionals as collaborative rather than negative and had enough information about their child's disability and services (see Chamba *et al.* 1999 for more detail). Parents who felt valued by professionals reported fewer problems than those whose contact with professionals was distant or strained. Parents who said they were well informed about their child's disability and about local services reported fewer service problems than those with unmet needs for information. Asian parents who needed an interpreter when talking to professionals reported slightly more service-related problems than those who could manage without such support.

Short-term care can provide a welcome break for parents and children (Baldwin and Carlisle 1994). Use of different kinds of short-term care also varied with parents' ability to understand spoken English. Parents with greater understanding of English were more likely to know that short-term care services existed and more likely to have their child attending these services. Again, this probably reflects the ability to negotiate access to services. More parents with little or no understanding of English reported that these services were not provided locally, reflecting doubt and lack of information about their existence.

In contrast to short-term care services, there was no association between ability to understand spoken English and support group membership. Overall one-third of the parents lacked knowledge about support groups, twice the proportion in Beresford's (1995) survey. Pakistani and Bangladeshi parents were least well informed about support groups. Only one-sixth of the Pakistani parents were members, compared to one-quarter of the parents from other ethnic groups. The most commonly cited reasons for using support groups were as follows:

- having someone to talk to in same situation
- finding out about local services
- finding out about benefits
- allowing the child to meet other disabled children
- finding out about the child's condition or about planning for the future
- improving their social life
- for Asian parents, meeting parents of same culture or linguistic background.

That support groups provided various benefits was obvious. Parents who were members were more likely to feel that their own and their children's needs were being met. Assistance with the following needs was strongly related to being a member of a support group:

- help with developing their child's physical abilities as much as possible
- help with developing their child's social and relationship skills
- the parents' need for someone to show them which services are available
- the parents' need for someone to look after their child at family and community events.

However, the limited information about support groups, coupled with the possibly limited availability of culturally appropriate provision, meant that the vast majority of minority ethnic parents were unable to take advantage of these benefits of membership.

Language, culture and knowledge

Use and command of languages is not separate from the cultural hues, sensibilities and stocks of knowledge which accompany their use. While there is much in common between different languages, languages also bring in train a range of different cultural assumptions about the world, how it is ordered, and the conduct of appropriate behaviour. Deaf people using British Sign Language, for instance, represent a good example of how language use gives rise to particular notions of identity which may mirror particular perceptions and expectations of welfare services and needs (Harris 1995; Ahmad *et al.* 1998). Possession of more than one language may enable people to move more easily through different cultures and, drawing on different stocks of cultural knowledge, better negotiate access to a wider range of institutions including welfare services (see Currer and Stacey 1986; Kreps and Kunimoto 1994).

This may explain why it was important for parents to use interpreters who spoke the correct dialect and possessed the requisite contextual knowledge of the child's impairment and available services (see also Chamba et al. 1998b). Many parents valued the opportunity that support groups provided to meet parents who shared their language, culture and religion. Some parents expressed concerns about cultural insensitivity of short-term care. The absence of lessons in Asian languages for their children in schools was also a source of dissatisfaction for some parents. This indicates not only the importance of language as an instrumental means of communication and acquiring information but also its significance in contributing to the cultural socialization of disabled children. This resonates with research on Asian deaf children and their parents' concerns about children acquiring their family language as part of cultural socialization (Chamba et al. 1998b; see also Ahmad et al., Chapter 5).

Discussion

Being able to use a language that one is competent in not only facilitates access to information but also represents an important principle of substantive citizenship. Language and communication concerns are especially relevant to a consideration of Asian populations' access to welfare services, because of varying use of English. Information about the child's condition, services for the child and support available for parents is vital for parents of disabled children. That it is often not available is well documented; this chapter shows that minority ethnic families are particularly deprived of such information. The task of caring requires access to a variety of informal and formal resources – material, social, emotional and professional support among these. Without access to appropriate information, parents and families of severely disabled children may cope without the guidance and support to which they are entitled and thus impoverish their own and the disabled child's quality of life.

Problems of understanding and communication with professionals underpinned many of the concerns reported by parents. Obstacles to effective communication may be faced even before diagnoses are made (Shah 1992; P. Turner and Sloper 1992; Atkin et al. 1998b; Chamba et al. 1998b) and continue to exert an ongoing influence throughout parents' contact with services, use of short-term care, access to disability benefits and ability to negotiate problems with housing as reported in the main study (Chamba et al. 1999).

There is an age gradient in the use of English among the Asian populations, with younger people having higher rates of fluency and literacy than older people (Modood *et al.* 1997). As parents of relatively young children, respondents in this study represented a younger sample than the adult population in their respective ethnic groups, but many still did not use English with ease. The need and provision of interpreters reflected parents' use and command of English but provision of interpreters did not meet all need. Families recognized the advantages of using professional interpreters. It helped them express their own views and eliminated the need to rely on family or friends. However, those who had experience of using professional interpreters reported problems, especially the use of difficult terminology, not speaking the appropriate dialect and interpreters not knowing enough about the child's condition or services. Interpreter or link worker schemes remain inadequate with users still relying on kin, including young children for interpreting. Where professionally qualified interpreters are employed, users have reported problems including delays, limited knowledge of the specific condition or inadequate matching for different dialects (Tomlin 1994; Chamba *et al.* 1998b; see also Atkin *et al.*, Chapter 7 in this volume). Atkin *et al.* note that often the affected children themselves provide interpreting between parents and professionals, an experience often distressing for the children and parents. There was still a considerable reliance on non-professional interpreters. Using unqualified interpreters raises ethical and practical problems and, despite being contrary to the Patients' Charter, remains routine practice. Many parents remained poorly informed about their child's condition and services for themselves and their child. This was consistent with links established in the study between poor use and command of English and benefits, dealing with living circumstances, problems in communication with and relationships with professionals, more service-related problems and knowledge or use of short-term care.

Conclusion

Parents with disabled children experience a variety of hardships (Baldwin and Carlisle 1994; Beresford 1995). The inability and unwillingness of services to equitably deal with minority ethnic parents, especially those who do not use English, exacerbates their plight. Our work shows that for many, attainment of such basic rights as information about their disabled children and entitlements to welfare for their disabled children and themselves remains impossible.

Acknowledgements

Our thanks to the Joseph Rowntree Foundation for financial support, the many families for their precious time and the Advisory Committee for sound guidance. The project was conducted jointly with Bryony Beresford, Dot Lawton and Michael Hirst.

Notes

1 The Family Fund Trust (FFT) is an agency (established in 1973) which distributes grants throughout the UK to families with a severely disabled child.
2 *Nam Pehchan* analyses South Asian names and assigns them to probable language and religious categories.
3 FFT Visitors are employed by the FFT to contact families to assess their eligibility when an application is made for material support.

7

Service support to families caring for a child with a sickle cell disorder or beta thalassaemia major: parents' perspectives

Karl Atkin, Waqar I.U. Ahmad and Elizabeth N. Anionwu

Recognition of the particular care needs of minority groups at the highest level of policy making has been described as 'something of a breakthrough' (Walker and Ahmad 1994), particularly since it occurs against a backdrop of often inaccessible and inappropriate service provision (Atkin and Rollings 1993). The difficulties faced by disabled and chronically ill minority ethnic people and their families in securing formal support are noted in chapters in this volume and elsewhere (Ahmad and Atkin 1996b; Atkin and Rollings 1996). The narratives of parents whose children have a sickle cell disorder or thalassaemia major reflect many of these difficulties (Aamra Darr 1990; Anionwu 1993; Midence and Elander 1994).

By presenting material from a project evaluating support to families caring for a child with SCD or thalassaemia major, this chapter specifically outlines the problems that parents face in gaining access to appropriate provision. In doing so the chapter helps identify potential needs, as well as the types of support that parents find helpful. More generally, the chapter contributes to the growing literature on care-giving and service support in relation to minority ethnic families (Atkin and Rollings 1996) and provides further insights for appropriate organization and delivery of health and social care to minority ethnic groups (McNaught 1986). Current writings on disability and chronic illness, both in their different ways, present individuals as active agents, exercising control over their lives. The disability movement constructs this active agency within a political framework (Oliver 1996), whereas those writing on chronic illness emphasize the role of individuals in interpreting and making sense of their illness within a social context (Conrad and Bury 1997). Both approaches, however, give primacy to the individual and their experience. At one level this is extremely important, especially since the voice of the individual is marginalized (Oliver 1996).

There is, however, a tension in asserting individual rights of disabled and chronically ill people and the primacy of their experience. The increasingly powerful critique from the disability movement, despite its obvious merits, tends to be dismissive of family care by arguing that policy should not endorse dependence on family care-givers but underwrite the independence of the disabled person (Oliver 1996). This approach is perhaps understandable, given that the state often advocates family care at the expense of considering how best to achieve optimal independence for disabled persons and their family (Twigg and Atkin 1994). Disabled people and their carers have to face the consequences of this and experience disadvantages that prevent them from enjoying the same opportunities as most other people. This would make disabled people and their carers as natural allies, rather than discrete groups competing against each other for limited resources, or the notion that carers are privileged by professionals or exercise undue power over the needs of disabled people themselves (see Chapters 2 and 3). For their part, carers' groups are perhaps as guilty in maintaining this opposition as disabled organizations.

Simplistic constructions of independence have thus been challenged (G. Parker 1993b). At its most straightforward, the provision of support to replace family care may run counter to what the disabled person wants. Disabled people rarely choose to reject the care of close family, for example, especially if they share the same household. The language of independence and control over resources becomes particularly problematic when applied to disabled children. This argument, although applying generally, may also have particular implications for minority ethnic disabled people and their families (Ahmad 1996). Members of disability movements have been slow to consider ethnicity and many of their arguments about independent living may have little relevance for minority ethnic groups. It is difficult to focus on the needs of the individual in isolation of the family and social context (Twigg and Atkin 1994) irrespective of ethnic origin (Atkin and Rollings 1996). Not only is the care of an individual negotiated within the context of obligations and reciprocities (Finch and Mason 1993), but also people rarely take decisions about their life and lifestyles independently of their families. More specifically, the influence of family members on each other and their different roles within their family have long been recognized as affecting the functioning of the whole family (Minuchin 1974). This does not deny the individuals' personal perspective nor does it negate their right to independent living. Rather it recognizes the role of family in shaping the experience of the individual (Midence and Elander 1996) and the important role of the family in supporting disabled and chronically ill people, especially children (Twigg and Atkin 1994). Both affected individuals and their families have to cope with 'disability' and 'chronic illness'; as Katbamna et al. (see Chapter 2) note, often the stigma and hardships are shared by both. This does not suggest a unified experience, as the implications of the impairment or illness can be very different for those who have the condition and those who provide support. Equally the distinction 'disabled person–carer' is not in any way absolute. Disabled people themselves may be providing many support or care responsibilities for their relatives. None-theless, each has their own distinct narrative that contributes to the politics of sickle cell and thalassaemia. This chapter focuses on the experience of parents of children with a sickle cell disorder or thalassaemia major in relation to health and other services.

SCD and thalassaemia: a brief note

SCDs and thalassaemia major are recessive conditions where individuals who inherit a deleterious gene from both parents develop the disease. In the UK the groups most at risk of SCDs are people of African Caribbean and West African origin. Thalassaemia is more likely to be found among people of Cypriot, South Asian or Chinese origin. The thalassaemia gene can also be found in people of African Caribbean origin and white British people. There are estimated to be between 6000 and 10,000 people with SCD and around 600 cases of thalassaemia major in the UK. There are, of course, many more carriers of these conditions.

SCD is an umbrella term that includes sickle cell anaemia, haemoglobin SC disease and sickle beta thalassaemia. Those with SCD are prone to 'sickling' of the red blood cells. This 'sickling' causes blockages in smaller blood vessels which can result in severe pain – often known as 'the painful crisis' – as well as anaemia, leg ulcers, stroke and damage to various parts of the body including the spleen, kidneys, the hips, eyes and lungs. Children are extremely vulnerable to strokes and life-threatening infections, such as pneumonia and meningitis. Treatment and care include the prevention of life-threatening infections, pain management and the avoidance of circum-stances that cause the red blood cells to 'sickle'. SCDs are variable, unpre-dictable and, at times, life threatening. Chapter 4 focuses on young people's experiences of living with a sickle cell disorder.

A child born with thalassaemia major is unable to make a sufficient amount of haemoglobin and needs blood transfusions every four to six weeks for life. The body's inability to excrete excess iron following these regular transfusions requires patients to inject themselves, with a drug such as desferrioxam-ine (desferal), using a battery operated pump, eight to twelve hours a day, five to seven nights a week. Complications of thalassaemia major include diabetes, delay or failure to enter puberty and infections, such as hepatitis C, acquired through blood transfusions. In comparison to SCD, the prognosis of thalassaemia major is more predictable and the condition more stable, although early death through non-use of the infusion pump is common.

This chapter complements Chapter 3, which considers attributions of cause for haemoglobin disorders, Chapter 4, which explores young people's experiences of living with sickle cell disorder, and Chapter 8, which focuses on the role of primary care teams in supporting carers.

Haemoglobinopathy service provision

Poor quality welfare provision often exacerbates the difficulties faced by parents of disabled or sick children (Atkin and Rollings 1996). Services for SCD and thalassaemia major, for example, have been described as erratic and lacking in coordination (Davies *et al.* 1993). Services that do exist have developed as much as a response to community pressure as to rational needs assessment or service interests among providers (Atkin *et al.* 1998a). The research on service provision to families with children with haemoglobinopathies documents a variety of problems, the consequences of which range from denial of information to avoidable suffering, stress and death (Aamra Darr 1990; Anionwu 1993; Midence and Elander 1994). These shortfalls in provision mean that patients with haemoglobinopathies and their carers receive poor information as well as inadequate treatment and support (Black and Laws 1986; Shackle and May 1989; Charache and Davies 1991; Anionwu 1993; Ahmad and Atkin 1996a; Midence and Elander 1996).

Access to information is a general problem facing all parents (SMAC 1994) and has particular significance in understanding how parents cope with a haemoglobinopathy (Ahmad and Atkin 1996a). Appropriate information can facilitate successful coping through improved understanding of the condition and its consequences, assistance in coordinating services and guidance on entitlements (Beresford 1994a, 1994b; see also Chamba and Ahmad, Chapter 6). People with SCD or thalassaemia major and their carers, however, often complain that they lack the most basic knowledge about the condition and express doubts about the ability, or indeed the willingness, of health professionals to provide such information (Aamra Darr 1990; Anionwu 1993; Midence and Elander 1994). Particular problems include inaccessible information given at what is often regarded by parents as an inappropriate time, an insufficient or rushed explanation of the condition and its implications for both parents and children, and the lack of opportunity to ask questions about the condition (Anionwu 1993). The lack of interpreting and translating services often compounds these problems for South Asian families (Atkin *et al.* 1998b).

Parents of children with a SCD report specific problems in adequate treatment of pain and criticize health professionals for not appreciating the severity of painful crisis (Murray and May 1988); Chapter 4 gives an account of problems experienced by young people with sickle cell disorder. Children, in severe pain, often have to wait for lengthy periods in accident and emergency departments before being admitted to the wards (Midence and Elander 1994), during which time they are often seen by inexperienced doctors who understand little about sickle cell (Anionwu 1993). These problems seem to continue when the child is admitted to a ward (Midence and Elander 1994).

For thalassaemia major, availability of beds for monthly transfusions is sometimes a problem (Aamra Darr 1990). Sufferers and their families are also unhappy about the time spent waiting before the transfusion goes ahead (Anionwu 1996b). Other difficulties include the timing of transfusions. Parents, for example, often have to take time off work to accompany children and would prefer transfusions to take place in the evenings or at weekends (Ahmad and Atkin 1996b). This would also ensure that blood transfusion did not disrupt a child's schooling. In addition parents complain that they are given insufficient support in the use of the infusion pump (Beratis 1993).

Many of the difficulties – such as lack of information, insensitive treatment and support by practitioners who know little about the condition – are also experienced by parents of children with other impairments or chronic illnesses (Baldwin and Carlisle 1994). Inadequate haemoglobinopathy provision, however, introduces the issue of racism (Ahmad and Atkin 1996a). The long-term neglect of these conditions by the British NHS, the poor coordination of services and the low priority afforded to haemoglobinopathies, including professionals' negative attitudes, are all pointed to by critics and users as indicative of institutional racism; many users recount incidents of individual racism (Anionwu 1993).

Within the context of the broad concerns outlined above, this chapter uses qualitative evidence to focus on the parents' relationship to service provision. Parental perspectives on issues relating to diagnosis are reported elsewhere (Atkin *et al.* 1998b) as are professionals' experiences of organizing services (Atkin *et al.* 1998a). This chapter continues by presenting the broad problems identified by parents and then discusses their experience of specific services.

The study

The findings presented in this chapter are drawn from a qualitative study of service support to families of children with SCD or thalassaemia major (Atkin *et al.* 1997). The study examined both mothers' and fathers' perspectives on the nature and appropriateness of haemoglobinopathy provision and related these to the views of service practitioners and managers. This allowed an understanding of the support that parents find helpful in fulfilling the varied and demanding tasks they face as well as the difficulties experienced by those attempting to provide such support.

The evaluation was based on in-depth qualitative interviews with 62 parents whose children (aged 1–18) had a haemoglobinopathy, including 37 parents of children with thalassaemia major and 25 of children with SCD. The sample included 34 mothers, 24 fathers and 3 guardians, drawn from the records of health professionals in the north of England. This represented an almost total population sample of parents with children within this age range, in the seven localities included in the study. Eleven of the families with a child with SCD were Caribbean in origin, one was Indian, one Algerian, one Nigerian and three were of mixed ethnic origin.

Of the thalassaemia major sample, fifteen families described their ethnic origin as Pakistani, one as Indian, two as Bangladeshi and two as East African Asian. To gain an understanding of services from provider and commissioner perspectives, we also conducted 51 interviews with key service providers, managers and commissioners in the same localities. The accounts of these practitioners and managers are reported elsewhere (Atkin *et al.* 1998a, 1998b).

The approach to evaluation adopted by this project required a methodology that could reflect the plurality of social reality and accept that different stakeholders utilize and adapt different discourses as they attempt to make sense of the world. To accommodate this, we used qualitative methods, based on semi-structured interviews. This approach is particularly recommended for the study of the ways that individuals express their understanding of themselves, in the context of their social, cultural and personal circumstances (Mishler 1986). A topic guide identified a number of key themes developed from a review of the relevant literature on haemoglobinopathies, chronic illness and ethnicity and welfare. Under each topic, particular probes were included to make the conversation more focused, detailed and concrete.

Mothers and fathers were offered an interview in the language of their choice and by a researcher of their own sex. Of the 62 parental interviews, 21 were in languages other than English, 19 in Punjabi, 1 in Bengali and 1 in Urdu. These interviews were conducted by interviewers fluent in the language of the respondent and knowledgeable about haemoglobinopathies. All of these interviews were translated, verbatim, into English and fully transcribed. Analyses identified key and subsidiary themes and the findings are located in relevant theoretical and policy debates.

The parents' account

We have identified the broad problems experienced by parents in their contact with health services, which include lack of adequate and accessible information; professionals not recognizing parents' support needs, poor knowledge of haemoglobin disorders among front-line practitioners and insufficient language support for those whose first language was not English. According to parents, these problems can characterize all forms of service provision that they are in touch with. Later in the chapter, we focus on the role of key professionals and agencies.

The lack of adequate and accessible information

Information not only is a practical resource but also has a symbolic significance (Beresford 1994a; 1994b). Obtaining information, however, was a problem mentioned by nearly all the parents in the study. Two shortfalls were especially mentioned: information about the nature and consequences of the condition and information about the support services available (see also Chapter 6). Their experience is similar to parents of children with other conditions and disabilities (Baldwin and Carlisle 1994).

First, most parents found it difficult to gain information about the consequences of SCD and thalassaemia major; we have noted difficulties experienced in relation to diagnosis and screening elsewhere (Atkin *et al.* 1998b). As we have seen, such a shortfall could have important implications for caring, because evidence suggests that the more that parents know about the condition, the easier they find it to cope with the consequences of the condition (Midence and Elander 1994). Elements of this emerged in the parents' accounts to the extent that information assumed both a practical and symbolic significance. Gaining information about SCD, for example, was seen to give parents an element of control over the condition. The unpredictable nature of the condition made such information especially important as parents used the information to introduce a degree of certainty into the prognosis. To be fair to the health professionals, some of the information needs generated by these parents could not be met: for example, given the variability and unpredictability of SCD a definite prognosis for SCD is not possible. Nonetheless, health professionals do not help their relationship with parents by appearing reluctant to provide information, giving information in impenetrable jargon, rushing explanations and providing information in abstract terms. Mrs Taylor, whose daughter had SCD, remarked: 'They don't talk to you, they don't talk to you, I mean they ask you questions. But they don't explain anything.'

More generally, parents believed that they had to be more proactive in gaining information from health professionals than they felt comfortable with. Other criticisms included explanations that were either difficult to understand or rushed, and the inability to follow up information and ask questions about the condition. Mrs Harding, for example, criticized the use of jargon: 'To be honest I didn't have a clue what she [the consultant] was going on about. I still don't. I could ask questions all right but I don't understand the answers.'

Mr Sol remarked that the consultant did not like to be interrupted and did not encourage him or his wife to discuss the condition. Rukshinda Daudji felt under so much pressure to take in information that she felt it inappropriate to ask questions.

Second, besides information about the condition, many parents commented on the difficulties of finding out about the support available to them. These difficulties seem common to all carers (Nolan *et al.* 1996; see also Chamba and Ahmad, Chapter 6). In this respect, many parents faced the circular problem of not knowing what they should know until they found out about it (Twigg and Atkin 1994). For these reasons, many parents relied on their own experience and contact with other parents to find out about services and benefit entitlements. Several recounted how it was only after many years that they discovered, often by chance, some potentially useful information. Suqlain Mushtaq, for example, complained about not knowing who to contact to ask for advice and gave the specific example of social security benefits: 'I mean basic things like, we're getting DLA [Disability Living Allowance] at the moment, but how many families actually know about that? We found out after a good four or five years that we could actually apply for this.'

Mrs Francis was especially annoyed at not being told what services are available and felt that it was wrong that she had to find out about such things on her own. Mrs Evans agreed and said that she 'shouldn't have to go looking for information'. The fact that parents of disabled and chronically ill children experience additional financial hardships is well recognized (Baldwin and Carlisle 1994; Beresford 1995). Recent work on minority ethnic parents with severely disabled children shows them to suffer even greater disadvantage than their white counterparts (Chamba *et al.* 1999).

Parents generally bemoaned the fact that contact with a health professional did not necessarily guarantee that they received their full service and benefit entitlement. Not surprisingly, parents said that they wanted a single accessible source of comprehensive information and this was the reason they valued their contact with the specialist worker (see pp. 117–18). Again this is an important theme of the more general caring literature (G. Parker 1993a; Twigg and Atkin 1994).

Recognizing parents' support needs

A common problem voiced by parents concerned the lack of general service support (see also Chamba and Ahmad, Chapter 6). Most parents felt that they had to battle constantly for adequate provision and recognition of their need; this added to the stresses of their caring role and is a problem noted in the general caring literature (Twigg and Atkin 1994). Specific problems mentioned by parents included the inability of health professionals to refer them on to other services, especially those outside of health care. Consequently service provision seemed fragmented to many families. As part of this, parents identified the attitude and incompetence of health professionals as one of the biggest problems they faced. Mrs Johns explained the problem: 'I think it's not the illness, it's the way people treat you, like, that's the biggest problem, how people treat you . . . Ignorance, yeah, but that comes from the consultants all the way down, do you know what I mean?'

Parents also noted the failure of service agencies to recognize their caring responsibilities and the difficulties they faced. Consequently, there were times when they felt no one understood their situation. These parents, like most carers, expressed a more general need to occasionally talk to someone about their current anxieties or worries for the future (Levin *et al.* 1989). Often they simply needed reassurance or advice on helping their child come to terms with the condition. However, parents criticized practitioners for not offering information and advice to assist parents. Often parents needed new information in response to the child's development, changes in the condition, or questions asked by the growing child. Many parents were frustrated that there was no easy way of getting information consistent with the changing needs of the parents and children. Mrs Wynn explained the problem: 'You go through agony. Watching them in pain and them wondering why it is happening to them. I mean what do you do when your child asks "Why can't I be like everyone else?" It cuts you deep.'

Nearly all parents agreed that it was difficult to obtain advice on how to support and encourage their children. Parents felt especially unsupported by health professionals, who they thought were quick to condemn parents for 'over-protectiveness' or 'unhealthy obsession' with their children's health, but often unable or unwilling to help or offer constructive advice. This is a common theme in the literature on haemoglobinopathies (Midence and Elander 1994).

Parents also felt that practitioners rarely recognized their wider family and employment commitments. Several parents experienced difficulties in arranging alternative care for their other children while visiting hospital. These parents remarked, however, that health professionals were largely unsympathetic to their problems. Employment commitments represented another problem. Attending hospital appointment could, in some cases, affect the parents' income. Several were paid by the hour, often supplementing their income with overtime payments; they therefore received no pay when they took time off from work to care for the child. As we shall see, the financial impact of looking after a child with a haemoglobinopathy makes such a loss of earnings especially difficult and this adds further to the pressures of caring. This seems a general problem among family care-givers (Baldwin and Carlisle 1994; see also Chapter 6).

Eight parents, mostly African Caribbean, explicitly mentioned the problems of racism in service provision. Many parents felt that identification of SCD as a 'black problem' meant that it received little attention. Mrs Prince felt that services available for what she regarded as a 'white genetic disease', cystic fibrosis, were considerably superior than those available to people with SCD. Mrs Francis commented that SCD would have received greater attention if it affected 'white' people. More generally, these parents also felt that services were not able to meet the needs of minority ethnic people. In addition to general neglect, Mrs Adams also identified incidences of individual racism:

I don't lightly say it but there are the nurses that I know, you know, have that attitude . . . In terms of, if I ask, I've got to ask very specific, very direct questions to actually get an appropriate response and I know that they know that I know. It's kind of that situation going on and otherwise you know, get very, very flippant answers, you know, or they do just enough that you know that they're not going to do anything extra. They just do the absolute minimum for Jane [daughter with SCD] and you know, I know which nurses they are and Jane knows and Jeff [husband] knows and it's just like, you know, just making clear in a very soft way that we know what's happening and they can think what they like.

We note similar criticisms from parents of children with thalassaemia major later in this chapter.

Knowledge of front-line practitioners

Lack of knowledge among front-line practitioners is a common feature of the literature on haemoglobinopathies (Davies *et al.* 1993; SMAC 1994; Anionwu 1996a; Dyson 1997) and of chronic illness in general (Green and Murton 1996). The parents' accounts generally confirmed this problem and described difficulties with most of the practitioners they had contact with. Parents often felt it necessary to explain the condition regularly to junior doctors and nurses. Parents also found that social workers and teachers were ignorant about the illness and its implications for individual and family life. Parents complained that this lack of knowledge added to the stresses of their caring role, making the situation more difficult than it need be. This is an issue that we explore further when we discuss specific services.

Language support

The problems experienced by parents were often exacerbated by a lack of language support for those whose first language was not English, a problem also noted by others (Atkin and Rollings 1993; Butt 1994; Walker and Ahmad 1994; see also Chamba and Ahmad, Chapter 6) and one that has particular relevance to families caring for a child with thalassaemia major (Aamra Darr 1990).

Many parents identified a lack of language support as contributing to their poor understanding of the condition, as well as adding to their sense of powerlessness and isolation. Parents often had to make do with unsatis-factory interpretation and translation support. Several parents complained that information was available only in English. On a more practical level, the use of family members as interpreters was often inappropriate despite it being common practice in many service agencies. Use of family members, for instance, could exclude parents from decision making, particularly those who allowed their child or spouse to translate for them. Salma Jan explained: 'Well the doctors there, the children are with me so if they want to ask anything they'll just ask the doctor. The children have grown up now there's no problem about English now. If they've got any problems they just talk about it themselves, *nobody tells me* [emphasis added].'

Parents also expressed concern about the pressures placed on spouses and children as they interpreted potentially stressful information while them-selves having to cope with it. In particular several mothers pointed to the problems that their husbands faced in simultaneously translating distress-ing information and coming to terms with it themselves. Fathers confirmed these problems and had particular difficulties in deciding how much they should tell the non-English-speaking mothers: often they wanted to 'protect them' from information deemed upsetting. However, this left mothers without crucial information about the condition, its consequences and implications for caring, information important for understanding, coping and caring. These mothers usually took on the main responsibility of care, yet were dependent on additional gatekeepers for information about the condition. Mothers whose child had SCD, however, had direct contact with practitioners. Consequently, many Asian mothers were left without a 'voice' and this, as we shall see, is why specialist workers, who shared the linguistic and cultural background of these women, were especially valued.

Nonetheless problems still occurred when interpreters were used (see also Chapter 6). Most interpreters, for example, had little specialist knowledge about thalassaemia and faced difficulties in interpreting clinical information and procedures, sometimes with unfortunate consequences. Robina Javed remarked that problems in interpretation meant that she did not understand that thalassaemia major was a lifelong condition. Nor did the Javed family realize that it was inherited until after the birth of their third child with the condition. Previous interpreters had emphasized that the child was born with the condition, not that it was transmitted through the parents. Other parents felt that the process of interpretation inhibited discussion. These appear to be generic problems in health and social care delivery and have been reported in relation to ethnicity and deafness (Ahmad *et al.* 1998; Chamba *et al.* 1998b) as well as literature on caring (Atkin and Rollings 1996). Health professionals, for their part recognize these problems and feel they lack the necessary skills in using interpreters (Atkin *et al.* 1998). Several parents also found the interpreter largely unintelligible because he or she did not use the same dialect as the parents. Practitioners were often not sensitive to these problems; at times their knowledge of users' language needs was offensively crude. Nurun Nissa Hussain, who spoke Bengali, was asked by her consultant if she could make do with Punjabi language support, because this was all the hospital could offer. Her protests that this was inappropriate were regarded as a sign of 'being difficult'. In the end she had to rely on her children to interpret for her.

Service provision

Having noted some generic issues, we now focus on specific services and professionals. Inevitably there is some overlap with the earlier discussion in this chapter.

Hospital services

Inadequate support in seeking treatment is a particular problem facing parents caring for a child with SCD or thalassaemia major (Midence and Elander

1994). Many of the problems described above were evident in the parents' relationship to hospital services. Overall, parents' experience of hospital services was mixed. Some consultants, for example, were valued for their medical competence, approachability and ability to listen. Others were criticized for not providing sufficient information, being unapproachable, using jargon and not recognizing parental needs. Parents would have also liked many consultants to be more sensitive to their worries and anxieties. Generally, many parents had little overall confidence in health care provision. This lack of confidence was especially evident in the accounts of parents whose children had SCD. Parents of children with thalassaemia usually expressed greater satisfaction with hospital services although, as we shall see, many remained unsatisfied with the quality of care, the time it takes to have the transfusion and the attitude of some staff.

Parents of children with SCD identified particular difficulties with inexperienced doctors and nurses who knew little about the condition; this caused them to doubt the quality of care received by their child. Mrs Hunter explained:

> The medical side should be a bit more informed about the illness so they can inform us about it, but I mean we've come across doctors, nurses who turn, we've asked them a question and they've turned round and said, 'Well I don't know anything about sickle cell.' So straight away, I mean I doubt them straight away. I think, 'Well why are they caring for my child if they don't know anything about it?'

Mrs Garner remarked that she had little confidence in the hospital doctors as they did not appear to know what they were doing. She added that the situation was made worse by the doctors' patronizing approach that they 'knew best'. Several other parents mentioned similar experiences. Mrs Prince sarcastically remarked that a doctor's ignorance of sickle cell was directly related to the arrogance that they assumed when talking about the condition.

The inexperience and ignorance of hospital doctors and nurses meant that nearly all parents whose child had SCD felt that they could not entrust the care of their child to hospital staff. Consequently, parents felt that they could not relax when the child was in hospital; many were reluctant to leave the child's bedside. This also explained the reluctance of parents to take the child to hospital in the first place, preferring to treat the child at home for as long as possible. (However, as we have noted in Chapter 4, treating a painful crisis at home is not an attractive option, and most sufferers require hospitalization for a major painful crisis.) Mrs Wynn said that she could never trust doctors because she has had to question too many medical judgements: 'And major decisions on how medication's administered to him in the hospitals and it's not done without my supervision and I'm with him 24 hours a day whenever he's admitted.'

The concerns voiced by parents were not those of 'over-protective' parents, as many could cite examples where things had gone wrong. Rukshinda Daudji related the incident of out-of-date blood being used during a transfusion:

'She, she was very poorly about five years ago. She was very, very poorly and she got blood transfusion and she was over dated you see and they didn't knew and then she had to, they had to give her 50 injections for that because it was all out of date, that blood transfusion.'

Another major problem raised by parents whose child had SCD, concerned inadequate pain control in hospital (see also Chapter 4). This was a particular problem for parents because pain is often described as the worst aspect of the condition, because of the practical disruptions that it caused, because of the parents' own distress at seeing their child in pain, and because it reminds parents of their child's vulnerability. The onset of pain also reintroduced the parents' concerns and anxieties about the future. Inadequate pain control in hospital exacerbated these worries.

Two themes emerge as parents explain the problems in controlling their child's pain. The first included the inflexible nature of hospital routines. Mrs Francis said: 'I think that's because they don't understand it and you know hospital, they go by routine. You get your tablet at 12 o'clock and they're not breaking that routine.'

Second, and more generally, parents believed that hospital staff did not understand the nature of the pain, often feeling that the child exaggerated his or her symptoms. Mrs Adams was especially angry that nursing staff felt that her daughter was exaggerating the pain:

I don't think they actually appreciate just how painful, you know, it [the painful crisis] is, you know, it's like 'Oh come on, you're a big girl now, you know, what's all the noise about?' And you know, I just, not wish it on them, I just wish they'd take their time to come, you know, to try and understand what it's about, or maybe if the pain nurses would actually explain how severe it is.

As we have seen in Chapter 4, inadequate pain control can reflect racial myths, such as the supposed tendency of African Caribbean people to have lower pain thresholds and the association of drug dependency with black people.

Most parents of a child with thalassaemia major expressed satisfaction with the child's admission for blood transfusions. No parents said that they had been turned away from hospital because of a lack of beds, a complaint common in other work (Aamra Darr 1990; Anionwu 1993). Many parents also praised the support and sensitivity of the hospital staff. Compared to SCD, fewer parents commented on the poor quality of care available to their child. Several problems, however, did occur and several parents had grave concerns about hospital treatment. Razia Khanum, for example, explained that the quality of care was so poor in hospital that she had no alternative but to look after her son while he was there: 'I don't care, if they're in a caring profession they ought to be caring.' Several parents also bemoaned the lack of flexibility in some settings, which made it difficult for them to meet their other commitments. Razia Khanum, who works full time, explained: 'But you have to wait for ages and sometimes they haven't got the blood or they haven't got his notes.'

The cost and organization of transport was a problem identified by many parents. Azhar Mujtaba said: 'We really need some transport . . . the factory I work in they won't give me time off to take Fozia [my child] to hospital . . . They [the hospital] say we've got no transport.'

Inadequate information about and support in the use of the infusion pump was noted by several parents whose child had thalassaemia. Health professionals, for example, were criticized for not explaining how the pump worked or its value to the child. Lack of information and understanding about the importance of compliance meant that nearly all parents had at times discontinued its use. Robina Javed's account was typical:

> As far as desferal's concerned, they [health professionals] didn't tell us that it ought to be continuous or regularly given, we didn't realize the effect it would have on the children if we missed desferal regularly. We didn't know and they did used to miss . . . on the surface we couldn't tell that it was having an effect, but obviously inside it was having a lot of effect.

Parents also complained that practitioners did not appear sympathetic to the emotional difficulties they face in using the pump and this (as we have seen) is part of a more general criticism concerning the inability of practitioners to recognize the parents' problems, particularly since compliance with chelation therapy caused considerable sadness and distress among parents. Farzana Islam summarized many of these difficulties when she remarked that inserting the needle for chelation therapy hurt her as much as the child: 'If something affects the children, it affects the parents before it affects the children. If the child has an injection in his thigh, first the mother has an injection in her heart, that's obvious.'

Primary care

Patients often bypass primary health care (Midence and Elander 1994), despite there being increasing policy emphasis on the role of primary care in haemoglobinopathy provision (SMAC 1994). Few parents in the study had an ongoing relationship with their general practitioner in relation to the child's condition. When contact was maintained, most used the GP to provide prescriptions for folic acid, penicillin and pain relief. Beyond this they did not expect their GP to be greatly involved in the care of their child. GPs share this view (Atkin et al. 1998a). Parents especially felt that GPs did not have specialist knowledge required to treat their child. Mrs Hampshire, whose child had SCD, explained: 'Well no, because I don't think he really knows much about it himself, to be quite honest with you.'

As long as GPs performed their instrumental role, most parents were happy. One-third of parents, however, had experienced specific problems with their GP. Lack of interest on the GP's part was a common complaint. Mrs Hunter described her GP as 'useless'. Other parents felt that their GP trivialized the condition and refused to take it seriously.

Specialist workers

Specialist workers or haemoglobinopathy counsellors are identified as fundamental in offering sufferers and their carers coordinated service provision, ranging from information about the condition, access to health care
and support with obtaining benefit entitlements (Anionwu 1996a). Parents
highly valued contact with the specialist worker, remarking on how the
worker had provided information, as well as more general practical, social
and emotional support. More generally, it was important for parents to
know that there was someone they could talk to who understood the condition and the problems they faced, especially given the negative experiences of service provision described by most parents. To this extent, specialist
workers represent an example of good practice, directly responding to user
needs and acting as a filter to other relevant services.

Mrs Prince, who was otherwise critical of services, spoke highly of the
specialist worker, praising her energy and knowledge: 'I don't know what
I would have done without [name of specialist worker] sometimes'. Razia
Khanum described the worker she had contact with as 'my guardian angel':

> It was like when, obviously [name of specialist worker] gives me a lot
> of support and I mean lucky she came around when she did. She came
> when he was about a year or one and a half, so I'd gone through hell
> before. Honestly, I mean she's heaven sent that woman. Yeah, I couldn't
> have coped without her, I mean I'd have done something stupid
> honestly . . . I needed someone like that, you know, not 'This is your
> child, this is his condition, bring him back to the hospital every four
> weeks'.

Mrs Sol described the counsellor as sympathetic and approachable, as well
as someone who got things done. Her husband agreed and described how
the counsellor had helped the family: 'Yeah, I think [name of counsellor]
has really has got the sufferer's interest at heart and, you know, she's going
to tell you what she can to help the kids, as much as she can, and try her
best to get what they need, you know.'

Many parents were specifically encouraged by the workers' knowledge of
the condition and their ability to offer practical advice. Parents also felt
that they could talk to these workers about their worries and anxieties. To
illustrate, Hajira Malik compared her relationship with the consultant to
her relationship with the specialist worker: 'She seems to understand as far
as I can gather, she seems to understand my situation. [Name of consultant]
is a bit harder to talk to for some reason.'

South Asian parents gained considerable benefit from sharing the same linguistic and cultural background as the specialist worker (also see Chapter
3). In most cases, the worker represented the parents' only contact with
someone with whom they could have a direct conversation. A common
language, however, was not the only issue. Several parents commented that
they were at ease talking to someone who understood their culture: '[Name

of worker] has been the best person, as she knows the culture as well and, you know, she can, she has this viewpoint from a Muslim background.' This comment relates to a discussion by Chamba and Ahmad (Chapter 6) that communication requires both a shared language and shared cultural context.

General problems mentioned by parents, however, included a lack of provision where a worker was off sick, left her post or was on maternity leave. The value placed on the service meant that parents keenly felt these gaps in provision. Furqan Nabi, for example, felt unsupported when the initial specialist worker left her post and did not know whom to contact for support. More generally, these specialist workers were not available in all areas. This reflects variations in haemoglobinopahty provision (Health Education Authority 1998) and meant that some parents experienced a better quality of support than others.

The role of social services

The literature notes the potential role of social service departments in supporting parents of children with a haemoglobinopathy (Ahmad and Atkin 1996a). The Children Act 1989 underlines this potential role and opens up a vast array of child-oriented social work for families with disabled children, including the provision of information, maintenance of a register of disabled children, assessment of need, advice, guidance and counselling and provision of social, cultural and recreational activities. The Act also makes reference to meeting the 'cultural and linguistic needs of ethnic minorities'. Evidence suggests, however, that social care agencies have little interest in haemoglobinopathies as they regard these as a health care issue (Atkin *et al.* 1998a), something confirmed by parents' experiences.

Few families had contact with social services and parents did not identify social care agencies as likely contacts for advice and support. Several parents felt that sickle cell disorder did not have a particularly high priority for social care agencies. Mrs Wynn attributed this to long-standing racism in social service provision, which meant that 'black' problems were marginalized. Other parents felt that there was a lack of resources. Mr Sol said: 'I think well, I suppose they would like to be sympathetic but you know, it's money when it comes to the end, you know, there's lots of people who need help and they've only got a limited budget.'

The few parents who had contact with generic social workers were not happy with the support they received. Social workers were particularly criticized for not having sufficient knowledge about haemoglobin disorders or for not understanding parental concerns. Balbir Singh, for instance, was disappointed by her contact with a social worker because he did not inform her about her benefits rights: 'But I feel social workers should tell parents what they can apply for and what's available, but they don't tell us that . . . I'm not asking for a guarantee that we will get help but at least to know what the possibilities are.'

Housing

Housing plays an important role in the overall provision of care (Chamba *et al.* 1999). Poor housing can threaten a child's health, as well as affect the ease with which parents meet the child's care needs (Beresford *et al.* 1996). This has particular implications for haemoglobinopathies. First, ethnic inequalities in housing are well established, with minority ethnic communities more likely to live in older, unmodernized, inner city housing which lacks household amenities such as central heating, washing machines and gardens (Skellington 1992; Ratcliffe 1996). Second, and more specifically, damp and draughty housing and lack of appropriate heating emerge as significant problems in caring for a child with SCD or thalassaemia major (Anionwu 1993).

About one-third of the parents reported problems with housing. Parents who lived in council housing, for example, felt that the housing department did not appreciate the housing implications of haemoglobinopathies and was generally unsympathetic to requests for more appropriate accommodation. Mrs Johns described her problems: 'I have had to have a major battle with the housing department. That was because they didn't recognize the condition . . . I had a major problem with them over that and when they found a house, we had steep steps to climb and it was damp and it wasn't warm.'

Help with the costs of care

Caring for a child with a haemoglobinopathy, as for other disabling and chronic conditions, has material consequences for the family (Black and Laws 1986; Ahmad and Atkin 1996a; Chamba *et al.* 1999). All but two families mentioned extra costs associated with caring for a child with a haemoglobinopathy; these included transport, heating, warm clothing, laundry, diet and telephone. Families were disappointed that little help was available with these extra costs, especially since many of these costs were seen as essential in maintaining the child's well-being. Consequently, the 13 families in receipt of Disabled Living Allowance (see Chamba *et al.* 1999) found the benefit extremely helpful. There were, however, geographical differences in the receipt of DLA. A family's receipt of the payment was often due to the involvement of a particular worker, usually a specialist haemoglobinopathy worker or local development worker. Consequently most parents in the same locality usually received or were in the process of receiving the benefit, whereas in other areas few parents had heard of this benefit (see Chamba and Ahmad, Chapter 6, for a discussion of the importance of information for parents of disabled children).

Further, most families who received DLA did so only after a long struggle and several appeals. The biggest complaint by families, initially turned down for the benefit, was that the Department of Social Security (DSS) representative did not seem to understand the consequences of the condition and often dismissed the parents' claim on the grounds of presumed inaccurate assertions about the condition. The illness, for example, was sometimes confused with the trait. Nor did the assessors seem able to understand the unpredictability of the condition. Several parents expressed particular anger over this, feeling that they were being denied their rightful entitlements. In some cases refusal was seen to belittle the parent's own caring role. More generally, most parents found social security entitlement complex and would have liked greater support and advice.[1]

Education

Interruptions to schooling are a particular difficulty facing children with a haemoglobinopathy. Parents are also concerned about whether teachers and other staff can cope with their child's illness. Parents often found that teachers understood little about their child's illness and therefore had to be proactive in educating teachers. Mr Sol, for example, provided his daughter's school with a dossier, which explained the condition and its consequences. The schools' response to the parents' input was mixed. Some teachers adopted a positive and sensitive response, others seemed to ignore the condition. Several parents remarked that the school felt that the child exaggerated the consequences of the condition. Mrs Francis, whose child had SCD, commented: 'They [the teachers] believed she was just, putting it on . . . I think they just don't believe because one time, one minute she could be fine, and the next time. They think it was an act.' This led several parents to worry about teachers' ability to deal with a painful crisis or other medical complications at school.

Many parents became especially frustrated at having to explain the condition to every new teacher the child had contact with and criticized the school for not taking more responsibility for informing staff. Mrs Leigh explained the problem:

> Sometime, like if I tell one, sometime if he's in another class, which I said to them, 'I don't think I should be telling each teacher, I think you should have got together in the staff room and discussed it'. You know, he saying, 'Oh Mr so and so won't let me go to the toilet mum'. And I say, 'I'll go to the headmistress' and she goes, 'I'll have a word with him', I says, 'Well wouldn't it be best, like if you did get them all together one day'.

Several parents went on to describe 'constant battles' with the schools as they attempted to convince teachers of the seriousness of their child's illness. More generally, it was rare for schools to contact the parents or health professionals for information about the illness. This led many parents to argue that health professionals should be more actively involved in educating teachers.

Besides teachers' lack of knowledge, another problem identified by parents concerned the lack of support during the child's absences. Several parents would have liked more advice from school on how they could teach their child at home. Other parents remarked that the school had frequently turned down their requests for extra homework to compensate for absences. Parents also worried and resented that the school had 'written off' their child. Overall many parents concluded that schools were poorly equipped to deal with children with a haemoglobinopathy, although their experience seemed no different from parents whose children have other chronic illnesses (Davis and Wasserman 1992).

Conclusion

On the whole, the parents' experiences substantiate the problems described in the previous literature on haemoglobinopathies (Midence and Elander 1994) as well as research focusing on other genetic disorders (Green and Murton 1996) and childhood chronic illnesses (Baldwin and Carlisle 1994). Parents, for example, face many problems in having their needs recognized, obtaining necessary information about the condition and sources of support, dealing with poorly coordinated services and dealing with often unsympathetic and poorly informed professionals. For many, unsympathetic professionals and ill-organized services are a hindrance in their caring tasks.

Ethnic minority status added to many of the parents' difficulties and distinguished their experience from parents whose child had other chronic illnesses. There was evidence, for example, that parent's choices were limited by the often racialized and stereotypical perspectives of service professionals or their inability to provide linguistically and culturally sensitive services. Many felt that haemoglobin disorders had the status of a 'black disease', and hence were marginalized both in terms of internal competition for resources and the seriousness with which the conditions were taken by health services. The ill-organized and ad-hoc nature of service development for haemoglobin disorders has been noted as a cause of considerable concern (Davies *et al.* 1993; SMAC 1994; Modell and Anionwu 1996).

The importance of well-organized provision by sympathetic, accessible and competent professionals is exemplified by the highly appreciated role of specialist haemoglobinopathy workers. Such workers were a source of vital information, a linchpin in coordinating services and enabling users to claim their entitlements, and a source of informal support to parents and children, particularly vulnerable parents (we have discussed how parents cope with their child's condition elsewhere: see Atkin and Ahmad 2000). Their important role was also clear in the systematic differences between support to parents who had access to such workers and those who did not. For example, parents who had access to such workers were much more likely to be receiving their benefits entitlements than other parents. Numerous studies are highlighting the need to provide a 'key worker' to families of disabled and chronically ill parents. Judging by the even greater hardships experienced by minority ethnic parents of chronically ill and disabled children, including experience of racism and language support needs, such workers would provide an important resource to families and affected children.

This study highlights difficulties faced by parents of children with haemoglobin disorders. Many of these difficulties have been noted in other research (Anionwu 1993; Ahmad and Atkin 1996a). However, importantly, it also highlights the value of well-organized support and the role of professionals in sustaining parents.

Acknowledgements

This project was funded by the NHS Executive's Initiative on Complex and Physical Disabilities. Our thanks to the many families for sharing their experiences, to health and other professionals for their time, and Marcia Hylton, Ghazala Mir and Shakeel Razak for assistance with the interviews.

Note

1 Assessment for DLA appeared haphazard. During the course of our work, we came across the case of an Asian man with sickle cell disorder who was supported in his application by the local specialist haemoglobinopathy worker. This worker was present for the assessment visit from a doctor. The doctor, wrongly, stressed that SCD was confined to African Caribbeans and that the applicant had no entitlement to DLA. The haemoglobinopathy worker's protests, herself a senior nurse, were brushed aside by the doctor. According to specialist workers, such erratic assessments were not uncommon.

8

South Asian carers' experiences of primary health care teams

Padma Bhakta, Savita Katbamna and Gillian Parker

In the mid-1970s Lamb (1977) argued that the aim of primary health care teams is to provide a comprehensive pattern of services embracing social and psychological as well as physical needs. Better patient compliance leading to a reduction of risk in ill-health (Department of Health and Social Security (DHSS) 1986, cited in Littlewood 1995), effective communication (Lawrence 1992, cited in Wiles and Robinson 1994) and the raising of standards (British Medical Association (BMA) 1974, cited in P. Pearson 1992) are among the identified benefits. Effective teamwork would benefit not only staff and patients but also carers.

However, there is ample evidence to suggest that carers' needs have not been met by primary health care teams (PHCTs) for a variety of reasons. Carers report that consultations with general practitioners are inadequate, where their concerns are not taken seriously (Moffat 1996). Lack of advice and information (Baxter 1989) and a lack of partnership between carers and professionals (Twigg and Atkin 1994) have resulted in carers missing out on vital services. When services have been offered, they have not always been appropriate or have lacked flexibility, with the result that carers have not been able to take up what was offered (Baxter 1989). On the other hand, carers may not be able even to access other services because primary care practitioners do not make appropriate referrals (Twigg and Atkin 1994).

The study

This chapter looks at South Asian carers' experiences of using services provided by primary health care teams. The methods employed for data collection are described in Chapter 2, which also lists the abbreviations used in this chapter (see p. 27). The first section of this chapter explores carers' positive experiences; the second focuses on their concerns and criticisms. The chapter demonstrates the importance of primary care practitioners in supporting carers and the difficulties faced by carers when such support is not forthcoming.

Carers' positive experiences with primary health care teams

As in other studies of caring (for example Allert and Gilbert 1994), carers reported that the general practitioner was usually their first port of call for health matters. This section describes the ways in which some carers felt that they were supported by their general practitioner or other members of the primary health care team beyond this basic clinical role. This support was of three distinct types: having access to information about benefits or services to help them in the caring role, professionals' positive attitudes and behaviour towards them and being recognized as carers.

Access to information and services

Information was directly provided either by the general practitioner or other members of the primary health care team and often related to diagnosis, nature of the condition, benefits advice and organizations that could support carers. Referrals to other services were made by the general practitioner, health visitor or community psychiatric nurse. Being able to access the community nurse meant that one carer was able to obtain incontinence pads for his son which previously he had to buy (PSM – FG). Referrals to social services opened up other avenues for carers in terms of aids and equipment or home adaptations. Some carers were pleased with the health visiting service in particular, regarding it a valuable source of information and support: 'Some of them have been brilliant, for instance my health visitor, she's been great, she's been supportive over everything . . . any problems I've had I've contacted her and she's done the running around for me' (PAKMF caring for son with cerebral palsy – ID).

More male carers than female carers were successful in obtaining information via the PHCT. This may be partly to do with gender differences within the different communities where men have greater experience of fulfilling such responsibilities. As Modood et al. (1997) suggest, more minority ethnic men than women are able to communicate effectively in English. Modood et al. (1997) also suggest that Indians and African Indians are more fluent in English than Pakistanis and Bangladeshis, with substantially fewer Bangladeshi and Pakistani women being fluent in English (see also Chamba and Ahmad, Chapter 6). Henley (1986) and Baxter (1989) have argued that inability to communicate effectively invariably leads to inability to access services. Our findings, however, suggest a more complex pattern with different groups being more or less successful in obtaining information about different issues. For example, Bangladeshi carers seemed more successful in obtaining guidance on how to care but had less success than other groups in obtaining information about their entitlements or services and equipment they could use to support them in their caring role. In Chapter 6, Chamba and Ahmad note that parents found it easier to obtain information on their disabled child's condition than on support available for the child or themselves.

Being able to communicate effectively with professionals meant that carers were able to obtain information on benefit entitlements, diagnosis and on caring. It also meant that carers were able to tell the professionals what they wanted themselves, without resort to interpreters (see also Chapter 6). The findings support the work of Ahmad *et al.* (1989) who report that South Asian people who have poor or limited fluency in English usually consult Asian general practitioners to overcome language barriers.

Carers who had their information needs met adequately were on the whole positive about PHCT services. General practitioners, health visitors and the community psychiatric nurse were the practitioners most commonly reported by carers as useful in helping them to obtain information.

Attitudes and behaviour of professionals

Carers also felt supported when professionals were kind, considerate or sympathetic towards them; this has also been noted by others (Chamba *et al.* 1999). For example, one Gujarati Hindu female caring for her adult daughter with mental health problems found the support of the community psychiatric nurse helpful in having her daughter admitted to hospital for treatment. This carer spoke little English and had little access to informal advice or support. She appeared to have been in a state of desperation. Because of personal knowledge of and hearsay stories about how people with mental health problems are treated, she feared that her daughter's condition would deteriorate or worsen upon admitting her to hospital. She was also battling with the fact that her late husband had requested that his daughter should not 'be given away to the hospital'. She said:

> So I was crying and she [other daughter] was crying and he [community psychiatric nurse] was being very sympathetic and really trying hard to make us understand . . . with great difficulty they took her [to hospital]. So me and my daughter went as well but I was worried about getting back . . . but he [community psychiatric nurse] understood and he said 'Don't worry, we'll get her admitted first then I'll come back and drop you back home'.
>
> (GHF – ID)

Carers talked about how 'good' a service was based on the attitudes and the approach that professionals adopted. The carer–professional relationships which carers described as successful were those in which the professional talked to and smiled at the carer. This included general 'chit-chat' as well as a genuine concern for the carer's welfare:

My doctor is very good, and half my problems are sorted out by just talking to him and the other half when I come home and take the medicine, I'm feeling much better, he's very good, I'm very happy with my doctor . . . I just go to the surgery and I'm feeling much much better, he's very friendly, very nice person.

(PSF caring for an elderly father-in-law
with incontinence – FG)

Chamba and Ahmad (see Chapter 6) also note the importance of a positive relationship between parents of disabled children and professionals (see also Chapters 3 and 7).

Appreciating the carer's role

The third positive aspect of PHCT professionals' relationships with carers was appreciation of their role as carers and the feeling that the 'door was always open' should they need help of any kind. A few carers were offered support, for example, in asking them to think over the option of residential placement for their relative. Although the option was not, by and large, taken up, it was the fact that their doctor had listened to their concerns and made some suggestions which the carer could consider which was felt to be of importance. The importance of doctors' being understanding and caring was more frequently reported by female carers.

Some professionals were clearly doing much to try and support carers. Carers, for instance, reported how their general practitioner did a home visit to explain the condition of the person they were looking after; this was clearly very helpful. Others were appreciative of their district nurse delivering incontinence pads, which saved a journey, or the nurse's willingness to change visiting times to suit the needs of the carer. One Bangladeshi female carer, looking after her son with learning disabilities, appreciated and valued the support of her health visitor, who had had information translated into the carer's language, and also because nurses, doctors and her health visitor would always praise her (the carer) for her efforts in caring.

Carers' negative experiences with primary health care teams

By contrast with the experiences summarized in the previous section, more carers reported dissatisfaction with the support they received from the PHCT. This covered the following areas:

- consultations with general practitioners
- attitudes of professionals towards carers
- access to appropriate services.

Consultations with general practitioners

Carers from all language groups were unhappy with consultation with their general practitioner, not only when it related to the person being cared for but also consultations for themselves. Carers were dissatisfied with their general practitioners for a number of reasons: because they had little or no time for carers and simply wrote out prescriptions; lack of explanation or inadequate explanations, for instance on issues pertaining to the cause of illness, diagnosis and prognosis; and the consultation being rushed. This meant that carers were sometimes unaware of the reasons behind their doctor's thinking and therefore unsure why, for instance, it had been suggested that medication for epilepsy be stopped (GHF – FG). More female carers than males felt consultation to be inadequate. This may be both because females were often the main carers and consequently had more dealings with the doctor and because male carers were treated differently by professionals. Atkin *et al.* (1998b) report mothers of children with haemoglobin disorders being less sympathetically treated than fathers.

Concerns about the cared for person not being taken seriously
Female carers in all groups expressed concern about not being taken seriously or believed (see Atkin *et al.* 1998a, 1998b; see also Atkin *et al.*, Chapter 7). In contrast, no male carers mentioned this. The main criticism was that general practitioners, and on occasions the health visitor too, did not take the carers' concerns about their relatives seriously. Carers reported having anxieties that 'there was something wrong' but having immense difficulty trying to convince professionals. Mothers of disabled children, daughters caring for parents and spouse carers all experienced difficulties of this sort.

A number of carers spoke of the 'struggle' between them and the professionals in trying to convince professionals that something was not quite right with their child only to have their doubts confirmed years later when a 'diagnosis' was finally made (see Atkin *et al.* 1998b). One Pakistani Muslim female caring for a 2-year-old, profoundly deaf child said:

> It took a long time . . . that put a lot of tension because to convince people, that was hell of a task . . . First of all because they [professionals] think, because it's your first child . . . it can't be, you know, it's always it can't be . . . They're always right, nobody at the higher, like hospitals and doctors they never want to know that they're wrong . . . but then again if you're a mother, you know your child, don't you?
>
> (PAKMF – ID)

In the most extreme case, one female carer described how it took her 13 years to convince her general practitioner that her daughter suffered from bouts of diarrhoea: 'She [GP] said, she didn't get it every day, when she does get it it's almost like opening up a water tap, it would happen on the bus or in school or anywhere' (GHF – ID). It was only when a new general practitioner had come to the surgery and she approached him that a referral was made to the hospital. After investigations it was found that her now adult daughter was allergic to wheat and had to have a gluten-free diet.

A few carers felt that although a referral had been made for a particular service, they continued to be passed from pillar to post and were, as one carer described it 'like a yo-yo, travelling back and forth from the hospital to the general practitioner'.

Carers' own health needs not being taken seriously
Most carers – male and female, young and old – felt that caring respons-ibilities had affected their health (see Katbamna and Bhakta 1998; see also Katbamna *et al.*, Chapter 2). Some carers suffered from specific complaints which could be managed with little medical intervention. They reported that they would visit their general practitioner only if they felt they had a clear health need or might need medication and were less likely to approach their general practitioner for psychological support.

However, a few carers did have conditions in need of urgent treatment which, left unattended, could have had serious consequences which would have ultimately affected their ability to care. Carers reported that their health needs were not taken seriously by their general practitioner, either because the general practitioner did not perceive the condition to be serious or because the general practitioner could not see the carer as a patient in his or her own right and linked symptoms to the carer's caring responsibilities. Hence, as one carer said, her general practitioner asked her how her husband was but did not ask how she was or how she was coping, even though she was the one who had gone to the surgery for her own needs (BMF – FG).

Female carers, in particular, spoke about their health needs not being taken seriously. It was only after they persisted or demanded blood tests or referrals, after making several visits to their general practitioner or after seeing a different general practitioner altogether, that they were able to get the treatment they needed. Some expressed the view that their concerns were not taken seriously because they were women and that their general practitioner attributed any problems to 'women's problems' or, as one carer was told, to age (being over 40) (see also Atkin *et al.* 1998b).

Lack of recognition of their caring role
Female carers generally spoke about the lack of recognition from their general practitioner of their caring role, reporting how difficult it was to convince their general practitioner that they were experiencing difficul-ties in caring. One carer related how she found it difficult to cope with her husband's bad temper and approached her general practitioner, who simply told her to continue looking after him. She said that when she was 'really fed up', she went to the doctor and told him: 'Look I am not just sick I am getting fed up care[ing] for my husband, I can't cope any more'. On that occasion her general practitioner said he was sorry for her but there

was nothing he could do. She went on to say, 'Sometimes my doctor jokes with me that I am still young, I have no problem, I can look after my husband' (BMF caring for husband who is physically disabled, has had two heart attacks and is a wheelchair user – FG).

Some felt that general practitioners focused on patients and therefore did not involve carers. Yet carers felt that they should be included in a conversation if they were the ones who would ultimately be involved in caring for the person. For example, a female carer looking after her diabetic husband felt that she should have been consulted on issues concerning diet and management of the condition in emergencies. Instead, the link worker informed her husband but did not inform the carer, who would ultimately be involved in cooking the food and would have to deal with her husband in an emergency. As a consequence, she was not sure what action to take in such a situation.

Lack of advice and information
Carers also felt that their general practitioner was not forthcoming with advice and information (see also Chapters 6 and 7). Concern was expressed in the following areas: lack of information about the medical condition and diagnosis, services available and how to access them, and how to care for or manage the person being looked after. Other issues such as the orange badge scheme (badge given to disabled drivers allowing parking in areas prohibited for non-disabled drivers) and benefit entitlements were also mentioned. Male and female carers' main concerns appeared to be lack of knowledge about what was actually wrong with the person they were caring for, which made caring more difficult (see Chapter 6). Those caring for relatives requiring a lot of 'hands on' care spoke about how they would have welcomed information or training on lifting and handling. These carers appeared to have learnt the techniques by watching others rather than through guidance and correct training.

Carers of relatives with mental health problems, on the other hand, wanted more factual information about the condition itself, how it could affect a person, how to manage behaviour problems and details about organizations which could support them and the person they were caring for.

Carers' concerns about relatives not being taken seriously
Carers spoke about how they had to be 'demanding' in order to be recognized and have their relatives' needs met. This meant being persistent and having the courage to speak up and express concerns to professionals, often on more than one occasion. One Punjabi Sikh female caring for her 17-year-old physically disabled son spoke about how she managed to get professionals to recognize her son's needs at a meeting she went to:

In these meetings they would ask me and my husband to come and bring my son with us. In these meetings they would also have a doctor present and myself and my husband would be busy looking after and

controlling our son . . . One day I said to my husband, 'Let him loose'.
This is the only way they [professionals] will get to know what he's
like and what his needs are and how I'm looking after him . . . First of
all he went to [the] doctor and he started playing with his instruments,
after that he started to mess around with [the] doctor's papers and
files . . . Within no time files were all over [the place], papers were all
over [the place], X had broken whatever he could get his hands on and
the doctor . . . said we would never ever have a meeting like this again.

(PSF – FG)

Some, however, thought themselves 'lucky' to be getting the services they
were or to have managed to get the services they wanted (see also Chapter
6). Some put it down to having a 'good' doctor who gave all the necessary
information and advice and made all the appropriate referrals. Others,
however, felt that it was best to be 'humble' and gratefully accept whatever
input was provided. This view was generally taken to avoid jeopardizing
the relationship with the general practitioner. Carers felt that if they pushed
GPs too much they might turn round and suggest that carers seek an alternative doctor, or restrict future home visits.

Attitudes of professionals towards carers

Male and female carers from all groups except Pakistani Muslim male
carers mentioned that they felt the attitude of doctors, nursing and reception staff to be 'off hand' (see also Chapters 3 and 7). Carers spoke about
how they were spoken to rudely or in a sarcastic manner, how they put up
with staff becoming angry or impatient with them, and how staff behaved
in an uncaring manner, often lacking sympathy for the carer.

General practitioners
There was considerable dissatisfaction about the manner in which general
practitioners behaved towards carers. A number of concerns were expressed.
For instance, one Gujarati Hindu female caring for an adult daughter with
learning disabilities said about her doctor's attitudes towards her: 'He will
say to you . . . What's the trouble? As soon as you walk in . . . He will say
to me, Now what's the matter?' (GHF – FG).

Some carers recounted their general practitioner's sarcasm at times, for
example, asking carers what medicine they would like prescribing, or whether
it was really necessary for the general practitioner to write a supporting
letter for a grant application for home adaptations. The issue of consanguinity was also felt to affect the manner in which general practitioners behaved
towards carers:

I'm most annoyed because the first thing they say is, 'Is it a first cousin
marriage? You've had one disabled child, then another.' He's a good
doctor, but because of his attitude, I only go when I really have to.
I feel embarrassed or ashamed almost. I feel that they must wonder

what kind of system Pakistani people have, and that we don't have any sense. They don't say it's our fault, but that's what they always ask. That feeling is there.

(PAKMF caring for severely physically
disabled daughter – FG)

Chapter 3 provides more detailed discussion of consanguinity and attribution of children's disabilities and chronic ill-health (see also Ahmad 1994).

Carers were unhappy about their general practitioners' making it obvious that they were very busy and did not have time for them, either by constantly answering the telephone in the surgery or making it clear to the carer, for instance on a home visit, that the patient and not the carer was the focus of the visit. However, one carer felt that the attitude of his general practitioner towards disabled people was equally bad. He said that he was told by his general practitioner not to bring his son to the surgery because he was disabled and 'that the other patients, well they would develop a heart problem just by seeing my son, they would be alarmed in the waiting room' (PSM – FG).

A number of carers were registered with Asian general practitioners. However, while one might assume that the lack of a language barrier could lead to improvements in communication and care, this was not the view of some carers. Pakistani Muslim carers were more dissatisfied than any other group with the services provided by Asian general practitioners (see also Ahmad *et al.* 1991).

Some carers felt that non-Asian doctors were better at treating Asian patients because they listened to their concerns and gave medication that helped them. One carer reported that she had changed from an Asian general practitioner to a white general practitioner because when she went to the Asian doctor he would not examine her or her daughter, he refused to visit the home, he would start writing a prescription straight away or would write a prescription over the phone, he would not listen properly to what she was saying and, if she said: 'Doctor, I haven't even finished what I wanted to say to you, he'd say to her "I haven't got time to listen"' (Pakistani Muslim carer looking after a severely physically disabled adult daughter – FG).

Gujarati Hindu carers, in particular, made more general comments with regards to both Asian and white general practitioners. They felt that general practitioners in general were budget conscious and therefore more focused on services for which they could claim a fee and therefore more reluctant to provide those for which they could not.

However, a few carers were more sympathetic about general practitioners' position, recognizing that doctors were under much pressure, with Asian general practitioners, in particular, having very large practice lists.

Reception staff and nurses

Surgery reception staff were also criticized for their ill-mannered and aggressive approach towards patients. Female carers spoke about how they found receptionists at their surgery to be rude and unhelpful, reporting that receptionists 'looked angry' (BMF – FG) or always spoke in an aggressive and angry tone. Carers could appreciate that receptionists had difficult jobs to do but at the same time felt that there was no need for them to behave in such a manner and vent their anger on carers.

On the whole, there were fewer criticisms of the nursing services on this particular issue although a few carers did report experiences with nurses who were rude or had a 'bad attitude' (PSM – FG).

Access to appropriate services

The literature review which accompanied this study (Katbamna *et al.* 1997) describes some of the difficulties that previous research has identified about carers' experiences of using primary health care services. Our study also revealed a number of difficulties.

Carers' awareness about the roles of professionals
It was evident that carers from all groups had very little awareness about the make-up of a primary health care team or what the roles of different professionals were. Some carers even mentioned that they were not fully aware about the role of their general practitioner. As a consequence, carers were not aware of the ways in which some services could help them and may thus have missed out on important support. There appeared to be more knowledge about the health visitors, among female carers, who remembered their involvement through their experiences of having a baby.

There was also considerable confusion as to who was actually visiting the carer. Many referred to 'the nurse' who, for instance, visited and provided a piece of equipment although, from their conversation, it was apparent that it was not a nurse but another member of the primary health care team such as an occupational therapist or physiotherapist. Some put their lack of awareness about different professionals down to not being educated or their inability to communicate fully in English. Considering the potentially large number of professionals involved with disabled people and their carers, such confusion is not surprising (Beresford 1995; Chamba *et al.* 1999).

GP home visits
Carers spoke about their experiences of home visits, made either by their general practitioner or the deputizing doctor, as being difficult or inadequate. Carers in all groups reported experiences of calling a doctor but being refused a visit or the doctor coming very late or not at all. While the doctor may have been right in not seeing a need for a visit in some cases, in others a visit was clearly needed. A Bangladeshi Muslim female carer described how her general practitioner did not visit her husband despite several calls being made. The husband was finally taken to hospital by ambulance after a 999 call was made by the carer's friend. The husband was found to have suffered a severe heart attack and was hospitalized for two weeks.

Deputizing services were also criticized for their very brief consultations. One carer reported that on one occasion the doctor had written out the wrong dosage of medicine for her daughter, who suffered from mental health problems (GHF – FG).

Failure to refer to appropriate agencies
Some carers had managed to get access to services such as district nursing but this appeared to be 'hit and miss', with much dependent on whether a referral was made, or whether carers were pointed in the right direction and able to approach organizations themselves. In a number of cases throughout all language groups, there was a clear need for a service but no referral or intervention had taken place, leaving carers very much on their own to shoulder responsibility. There appeared to be a need for the following services in particular: occupational therapy, physiotherapy, nursing services, speech therapy, bathing assistance and home help services. One carer whose son's disabilities were not 'obvious' reported having no input at all: 'We're not receiving any services at all. Just because you can't see his disability, doesn't mean he hasn't got one' (PAKMF caring for a son who was deaf and had behaviour problems – FG).

In one case, a female carer with bad eyesight was in need of an eye operation. She was told, in the first instance, that they would not operate because 'you're looking after your husband and he won't have a carer'. She was then told that the operation would be done, but only if she would refrain from physical exertion, such as bending. The carer agreed, but: 'There wasn't anyone else to look after him ... I had to more or less lie to them to get the operation done. They told me that for three months I couldn't really do anything for him, but I had to, I couldn't just ignore him' (PSF caring for husband with a stroke – ID).

In this instance, services would have been required only on a temporary basis; referral to the nursing services or social worker for temporary input would surely have been appropriate.

In another case, a Gujarati Hindu elderly male carer looking after his wife with osteoarthritis spoke of his experiences when his wife arrived home after discharge from hospital following a fall. He said he was managing the house and looking after his wife, but after discharge found it very hard to cope with bathing his wife, for which he requested support:

I told them my main problem was to bath my wife right now. 'We will send a nurse who will train you to do baths for your wife, how you can manage [bathing her] easily, how you can get her to sit comfortably and to make her stand up' and all that. I told them that I've been doing that for the last twenty years, I have had experience, but what I'm asking is whether you people can come and do it for me, now I'm having problems.
(GHM – FG)

A Punjabi Sikh female caring for her elderly father-in-law spoke about how she managed eventually to get incontinence pads through the health centre, after finding out about the service from the wife of her husband's nephew. Despite her general practitioner being aware of her father-in-law's incontinence problem, he had not made a referral.

General practitioners' own beliefs were also thought to influence whether carers were able to gain access to services or not (see Atkin *et al.* 1998b; see also Ahmad *et al.*, Chapter 3). Some female carers, in desperation, would have liked their adult disabled daughters sterilized, because of the difficulty of caring for them during menstruation. One Gujarati Hindu female carer was told by her general practitioner that surgery could not be done, and that it would be a sin to do so in any case. Why surgery was not possible was not adequately explained and the carer was left with the added guilt for requesting a procedure which the doctor clearly regarded as unethical. Nor was the carer referred to a support group or a social worker with a view to increasing the support she was receiving. Instead the doctor told her that 'rules like that', to allow such surgery, did not exist, but if she wanted to proceed then she would have to contact the social worker. She spoke to the social worker, who in turn said that she should speak to the doctor.

Difficulties with reception staff
Carers experienced a number of difficulties in getting in touch with their general practitioner and these complaints were often directed at reception staff who were thought to 'block' access. Carers complained about the length of time they had to wait to speak to the doctor over the telephone or not being able to speak to the doctor at all.

Inadequacies in the appointment system at the surgery meant that carers' needs were not considered and they had lengthy waits (see Chamba *et al.* 1998b, for a discussion). Some reported having to wait up to a week or more to see their general practitioner. Both male and female carers suggested the need for a more flexible appointment system which was geared towards meeting the needs of carers.

In several cases there were examples of receptionists simply not appearing to understand the circumstances in which carers lived:

> My little girl had a heart operation last year. It was very difficult, because I had no phone, and she fell ill. It was snowing outside. I had to walk all the way, carrying my daughter to the surgery. When I got there, the secretary [receptionist] sent me back home, saying, 'Make an appointment over the phone, and then come back' . . . Believe me. I came home crying.
>
> (PAKMF – ID)

Physical access to the surgery
Even where carers were able to negotiate their way past receptionists, issues of physical access sometimes impeded their ability to see the GP. Some carers in the study were involved in caring for very disabled relatives. Inevit-

ably, this made it more difficult if they were unable to get into the surgery because there were no appropriate access facilities. There were reports of surgery doors not being wide enough for wheelchairs or the surgery having too many stairs, which meant that the person being looked after could get to the waiting room only if the carer carried them up the stairs. One carer related how her doctor would not visit her son, who had learning disabilities, at home, but the son was not able to use the surgery because it had too many stairs. As a result, her doctor would write out prescriptions without seeing her son. This she felt to be unsatisfactory (PAKMF – FG).

Inappropriate or inflexible nursing services
Relatively few carers had any knowledge of community-based nursing services and even fewer any experience of them. The main comments made by those who were aware of them were about their cultural appropriateness and flexibility. Some Muslim carers, for example, said that they preferred not to use nursing services as they felt that cultural and religious rules of hygiene would not be followed. Carers were unwilling to request support when they knew that services could not meet such needs: 'What [can] people from outside do for him [husband]? I have to help him for washing [his feet] five times a day, who will come to help him five times a day?' (BMF – FG). This was a reference to ablution requirements for the five daily prayers for Muslims.

Some Gujarati Hindu carers, by contrast, were prepared to accept the support but still found nursing staff lacking in knowledge about cultural values. One, caring for her husband's grandmother, spoke about the views of the nursing staff she was in contact with:

> The nurse also thinks it is strange what we consider cleaning, not only the teeth but the tongue as well is very important . . . The nurses don't understand our culture. The other thing is, they think [X] should be wearing jogging suit because it would be easier to undress and dress her. They feel it will be easier for [X] to walk and be more comfortable than wearing a sari . . . The nurses think that's a lot better than trying to put on a sari because it's easier. So their values and views are different from ours but obviously that isn't right. It's strange to suggest even that an old lady like that should be, should wear jogging pants because, you know, that's not how we dress our people.

Lack of flexibility was reported by some carers who had used the services. Carers talked about how nurses often arrived too early; for example, nurses offered to come at 8 or 9 o'clock to put the patient to bed. This was often too early for the carer's relative and thus the carer continued without help. Other problems included arriving unexpectedly without calling, not calling to say why they were not coming to visit, delays in receiving the service once a referral had been made, not returning calls, or just the general feeling that receiving the service was more trouble than it was worth:

We have to be with the nurse when she is giving my [X] a bath. We have to be with her all the time. We keep everything ready before the bath, you know, all her clothes and everything is left ready for the nurse. So what happens at the moment is while she is giving her a bath you just stand around, you just have to hang around waiting. You can't just disappear. So, I feel I'm tied up because you just wait for the nurse to finish . . . the nurse feels she can't cope on her own so she needs help from us.

(GHF caring for husband's grandmother – ID)

Racism

The issue of implicit and explicit racism within the health services was explored in some detail in the literature review carried out as part of this project (Katbamna *et al.* 1997; see also Chapters 3 and 7). In this study, carers from all groups, other than Pakistani Muslims, referred directly to the issue, but particularly Bangladeshi Muslim and Gujarati Hindu carers.

One Gujarati Hindu male carer felt that Asian people were stereotyped by professionals, for instance, as all being unable to speak English. He felt that even though it might be the case that some Asian people are unable to communicate in English, interpreting and translating services did exist which should be used more frequently by professionals. It was also felt that services were not provided or were refused because 'colour was bound to be an issue' (GHF – FG) (see also Chapters 3 and 7). Others felt that white people received more and better services and support because people from South Asian communities were less aware of what was available and how to get access to it.

Bangladeshi Muslim female carers felt that just being Bangladeshi meant that they were not given any respect or valued by professionals, be it in a surgery or hospital setting. The conversation in one Bangladeshi Muslim female focus group illustrates this perception:

F1: They [receptionists] never want to help, their attitude is very bad, they're always cross with us, only the Bengali link worker is helpful, nobody else in the surgery . . . We live in this country, they also live in this country, but the people who work in [the] surgery they don't want to realize it. They always want to ignore us. They look us other way. They behave with us like they don't like us.

F2: The person who works in the GP surgery they always give priority to other people, not the Bengali people. Sometimes we have to wait a long time but they don't care, they always give chances to other people, not the Bengali people like us.

F3: They always look angry when they talk to us. They seem friendly to other people, but when they talk to us they look very angry. I don't know why.

Conclusion

Although some carers were positive about the PHCT in terms of receiving information and professionals behaving in a caring manner and recognizing the work of carers, the findings demonstrate that many aspects of services within primary health care are perceived as largely inadequate in meeting carers' needs. Inadequacies were identified in two particular areas: consultations, including information and advice giving, and access to and experiences of primary health care services.

Carers from all language groups were unhappy with consultations with their general practitioner, with more female carers than male carers reporting dissatisfaction. Consultations were reported to be rushed and inadequate, where general practitioners gave little or no explanation and often carers' questions or anxieties were left unaddressed or were not taken seriously. General practitioners were perceived to be more concerned about the disabled relatives and therefore did not include or involve carers in conversations and decision-making processes. Carers experienced impatience, sarcasm and rudeness, both from GPs and from other PHCT members, usually receptionists. It was thus the quality of interactions rather than their frequency that caused distress.

General practitioners and other members of the primary health care team have a responsibility towards not only patients but also their carers; ensuring that carers' well-being is maintained helps them to continue caring and provide high quality support to the disabled relative. This requires consultation to be sensitive to carers' concerns, allowing them, for a short time, to be the focus of attention. Consultations in which the needs and concerns of carers are valued and recognized would be in everyone's interests, not least through reducing the need for making repeated visits. Support services which let carers know that they have not been forgotten and that help is at hand do not have to revolve around the GP exclusively. Other primary health care staff can provide a vital service in providing advice and information to support carers. Often carers did not know what was actually wrong with the person they were caring for, were not aware about the availability of services (including nursing services) or their benefit entitlements (see also Chapters 3, 6 and 7). This inevitably made caring more difficult for them. Those carers that did have contact with nursing services found them to be lacking in flexibility and, in some cases, unresponsive to their cultural needs.

Nurses, in particular, could work collaboratively with general practitioners to ensure that carers' needs are regularly reviewed and monitored. This would prevent carers from getting lost in the system (particularly those who do not have frequent contact with primary health care services). Again it seems likely that intervention of this sort might prevent or delay greater costs by averting crises. This requires at least partial refocusing of services away from high priority crisis intervention towards preventive maintenance. Thus not only those carers with the most pressing need or experiencing a 'crisis' would have access to services, but also those who appear to be managing would also be offered necessary support and their situation monitored. As Twigg (1989: 64) suggests, 'a policy targeted on the prevention of the marginal erosion of care may therefore find itself focusing resources on some very *lightly burdened*, and relatively *unstressed* carers' (original emphasis) who have yet to reach this turning point, deciding whether to continue caring or not.

Often general practitioners' own perspectives on carers' needs and appropriate action disadvantaged carers through refusal to provide a service, poor quality of service, unsympathetic approach to the carer or their disabled relative, or failure to refer to other appropriate services. Other research shows that GPs' decision making is influenced by stereotypes of users' gender, ethnicity or social class (Macintyre 1977; Ahmad 1993; Atkin *et al.* 1998a, 1998b; see also Chapter 3). Primary health care teams need to ensure that minority ethnic users are not disadvantaged because of racist assumptions about need or deservingness.

Carers from all language groups spoke about their experiences of calling their general practitioner and either being refused a home visit or the doctor calling very late or not at all. Many carers were lacking information and advice about what to do in an emergency situation. General practitioners may be right in refusing a home visit at times, but it was apparent in a number of cases that there was a genuine need for a home visit and in some cases an urgent need. Carers resorted to calling for an ambulance in order to get treatment but this could have been avoided in some cases if they had known more about what to do in an emergency situation (for example if a diabetic person has a hypoglycaemic attack) and had been better informed about how to manage certain ailments and conditions which are often regarded as 'trivial'. Helping carers to recognize when it is and when it is not appropriate to request a home visit, again, can only benefit both sides. Other problems included poor access due to unsympathetic receptionists and physical inaccessibility of the surgery for carers or their disabled relatives.

In summary, the needs of carers could be improved through a variety of means. Some would involve very little cost, such as recognizing and valuing carers' concerns. However, as Twigg and Atkin (1994: 146) have argued, 'not all needs can be met by greater sensitivity and awareness. Sometimes carers simply need services'. Our study shows that primary health care professionals can be a considerable resource to Asian carers. However, too often, carers face varied and considerable barriers to adequate support from primary health care. And because of such barriers, they are denied both primary care support and access to other services for which primary care professionals act as gatekeepers.

Acknowledgements

This project was supported by the NHS Executive's Initiative on Physical and Complex Disability.

References

Ahmad, W.I.U. (ed.) (1993) *'Race' and Health in Contemporary Britain*. Buckingham: Open University Press.

Ahmad, W.I.U. (1994) Reflections on the consanguinity and birth outcome debate, *Journal of Public Health Medicine*, 16, 423–8.

Ahmad, W.I.U. (1996) Family obligations and social change in Asian communities: implications for community care, in W.I.U. Ahmad and K. Atkin (eds) *'Race' and Community Care*. Buckingham: Open University Press.

Ahmad, W.I.U. and Atkin, K. (1996a) Ethnicity and caring for a disabled child: the case of children with sickle cell or thalassaemia, *British Journal of Social Work*, 26, 755–75.

Ahmad, W.I.U. and Atkin, K. (eds) (1996b) *'Race' and Community Care*. Buckingham: Open University Press.

Ahmad, W.I.U. and Husband, C. (1993) Religious identity, citizenship and welfare: the case of Muslims in Britain, *American Journal of Islamic Social Science*, 10, 217–33.

Ahmad, W., Kernohan, E. and Baker, M. (1989) Patients' choice of general practitioner: influence of patients' fluency in English and the ethnicity and sex of the doctor, *Journal of the Royal College of General Practitioners*, 39, 153–5.

Ahmad, W.I.U., Baker, M.R. and Kernohan, E.E.M. (1991) General practitioners' views about Asian and non-Asian patients, *Family Practice*, 8(1), 52–6.

Ahmad, W., Darr, A., Jones, L. and Nisar, G. (1998) *Deafness and Ethnicity: Services, Policy and Politics*. Bristol: Policy Press and Joseph Rowntree Foundation.

Ahmed, L. (1992) *Women and Gender in Islam: Historical Roots of a Modern Debate*. New Haven, CT and London: Yale University Press.

Allert, A. and Gilbert, P. (1994) *Lewisham Black Mental Health Users and Carers Project*. London: Lewisham and Guy's Mental Health NHS Trusts.

Anderson, O., Bradley, L.A., Young, L.D. and McDaniel, L.K. (1985) Rheumatoid arthritis: review of psychological factors related to aetiology, effects and treatment, *Review of Psychology*, 98, 358–87.

Andrews, G. (1991) *Citizenship*. London: Lawrence and Wishart.

Anionwu, E. (1993) Sickle cell and thalassaemia: community experiences and official response, in W.I.U. Ahmad (ed.) *'Race' and Health in Contemporary Britain*. Buckingham: Open University Press.

Anionwu, E. (1996a) Ethnic origin of sickle cell and thalassaemia counsellors: does it matter?, in D. Kelleher and S. Hillier (eds) *Researching Cultural Differences in Health*. London: Routledge.

Anionwu, E. (1996b) Sickle cell and thalassaemia: some priorities for nursing, *Journal of Advanced Nursing*, 23(5), 853–6.

Anwar, M. (1977) *The Myth of Return: Pakistanis in Britain*. London: Heinemann.

Arber, S. and Gilbert, N. (1989) Men: the forgotten carers, *Sociology*, 23(1), 111–18.

Arber, S., Gilbert, N. and Evandrous, M. (1988) Gender, household composition and receipt of domiciliary services by elderly disabled people, *Journal of Social Policy*, 17(2), 153–75.

Atkin, K. (1991) Health, illness, disability and black minorities: a speculative critique of present-day discourse, *Disability, Handicap and Society*, 6(1), 37–48.

Atkin, K. and Ahmad, W.I.U. (1998) *Ethnicity and Disability: The Experience of Young People with a Sickle Cell Disorder or Thalassaemia*. Final report submitted to the National Lottery Charities Board. Leeds: Centre for Research in Primary Care, University of Leeds.

Atkin, K. and Ahmad, W.I.U. (2000) Family caregiving and chronic illness: how parents cope with a child with a sickle cell disorder or thalassaemia, *Health and Social Care in the Community*, 8(1).

Atkin, K. and Ahmad, W.I.U. (in press) Pumping iron: compliance with chelation therapy among young people who have thalassaemia, *Sociology of Health and Illness*.

Atkin, K. and Rollings, J. (1993) *Community Care in a Multi-Racial Britain: A Critical Review of the Literature*. London: HMSO.

Atkin, K. and Rollings, J. (1996) Looking after their own? Family care-giving Asian and Afro-Caribbean communities, in W.I.U. Ahmad and K. Atkin (eds) *'Race' and Community Care*. Buckingham: Open University Press.

Atkin, K., Ahmad, W.I.U. and Anionwu, E. (1997) *An Evaluation of Service Support to Families of Children with Sickle Cell Disorder or Thalassaemia*. Final report to NHS Programme on Physical and Complex Disability. Bradford: Ethnicity and Social Policy Research Unit, University of Bradford.

Atkin, K., Ahmad, W.I.U. and Anionwu, E. (1998a) Service support to families caring for a child with a sickle cell disorder or thalassaemia, *Health*, 2(3), 305–27.

Atkin, K., Ahmad, W.I.U and Anionwu, E. (1998b) Screening and counselling for sickle cell disorders and thalassaemia: the experience of parents and health professionals, *Social Science and Medicine*, 47(11), 1639–51.

Badat, H. and Whall-Roberts, D. (1994) *Bridging the Gap: Creating Services for Deaf People from Ethnic Minority Communities*. London: Royal National Institute for the Deaf.

Baker, M.R., Bandranayake, R. and Schweiger, M.S. (1984) Differences in uptake of immunisation among ethnic groups, *British Medical Journal*, 288, 1075–8.

Baldwin, S. and Carlisle, J. (1994) *Social Support for Disabled Children and their Families*. London: HMSO.

Baxter, C. (1989) *Cancer Support and Ethnic Minority and Migrant Worker Community*. London: Cancerlink.

Begum, N. (1992) *Something to be Proud of: The Lives of Asian People and Carers in Waltham Forest*. London Borough of Waltham Forest: Race Relations Unit and Disability Unit.

Begum, N., Hill, M. and Stevens, A. (eds) (1994) *Reflections: The Views of Black Disabled People on their Lives and Community Care*. London: Central Council for Education and Training in Social Work.

Beratis, S. (1993) Psycho-social status in pre-adolescent children with beta thalassaemia, *Journal of Psychosomatic Research*, 37(3), 271.

Beresford, B. (1994a) *Positively Parents: Caring for a Severely Disabled Child.* London: HMSO.

Beresford, B. (1994b) Resources and strategies: how parents cope with the care of a disabled child, *Journal of Child Psychology and Psychiatry*, 35(1), 171–209.

Beresford, B. (1995) *Expert Opinions: A National Survey of Parents Caring for a Severely Disabled Child.* Bristol: Policy Press.

Beresford, B., Sloper, P., Baldwin, S. and Newman, T. (1996) *What Works in Services for Families with a Disabled Child?* Essex: Barnardo's.

Bhalla, A. and Blakemore, K. (1981) *Elderly of the Minority Ethnic Groups.* Birmingham: All Faiths for One Race.

Bhopal, R. (1986) Asian's knowledge and behaviour on preventive health issues, *Community Medicine*, 8, 315–25.

Black, J. and Laws, S. (1986) *Living with Sickle Cell Disease: An Inquiry into the Need for Health and Social Service Provision for Sickle Cell Sufferers in Newham.* London: Sickle Cell Society.

Bould, M. (1990) Trapped within four walls, *Community Care*, 19 April, 810.

Bowler, I. (1993) 'They're not the same as us': midwives' stereotypes of South Asian women, *Sociology of Health and Illness*, 15, 157–78.

Bradby, H. (1996) Genetics and racism, in T. Marteau and M. Richards (eds) *The Troubled Helix: Social and Psychological Implications of the New Human Genetics.* Cambridge: Cambridge University Press.

Brah, A. (1992) Women of South Asian origin in Britain: issues and concerns, in P. Braham, A. Rattansi and R. Skellington (eds) *Racism and Antiracism: Inequalities, Opportunities and Policies.* London: Sage/The Open University.

Brannen, J., Dodd, K., Oakley, A. and Storey, P. (1994) *Young People, Health and Family Life.* Buckingham: Open University Press.

Briggs, A. and Oliver, J. (1985) *Caring.* London: Routledge and Kegan Paul.

British Medical Association (BMA) (1974) *Primary Health Care Teams.* London: BMA.

Bury, M. (1991) The sociology of chronic illness, *Sociology of Health and Illness*, 13(4), 451–68.

Butt, J. (1994) *Same Service or Equal Service?* London: HMSO.

Carby, H. (1982) 'White women listen!' Black feminism and the boundaries of sisterhood, in Centre for Contemporary Cultural Studies (eds) *The Empire Strikes Back.* London: Hutchinson.

Cashmore, E. and Troyna, B. (1990) *Introduction to Race Relations.* Basingstoke: Falmer Press.

Centre for Contemporary Cultural Studies (CCCS) (eds) (1982) *The Empire Strikes Back.* London: Hutchinson.

Chamba, R., Ahmad, W.I.U., Darr, Aliya and Jones, L. (1998a) Education of Asian deaf children, in S. Gregory, P. Knight, W. McCrackon, S. Powers and L. Watson (eds) *Education of Deaf Children.* London: David Fulton.

Chamba, R., Ahmad, W.I.U. and Jones, L. (1998b) *Improving Services for Asian Deaf Children: Parents' and Professionals' Perspectives.* Bristol: Policy Press.

Chamba, R., Ahmad, W.I.U., Hirst, M., Lawton, D. and Beresford, B. (1999) *On the Edge: Minority Ethnic Families Caring for a Severely Disabled Child.* Bristol: Policy Press.

Charache, S. and Davies, S.C. (1991) Teaching both the management and the molecular biology of sickle cell disease, *Academic Medicine*, 66(12), 48–9.

Charlesworth, A., Wilkin, D. and Durie, A. (1984) *Carers and Services: A Comparison of Men and Women Caring for Dependent Elderly People*. Manchester: Equal Opportunities Commission.

Chitty, L.S. and Winter, R.M. (1989) Peri-natal mortality in different ethnic groups, *Archives of Disease in Childhood*, 64, 1036–41.

Confederation of Indian Organisations (1987) *Double Bind: To be Disabled and Asian*. London: Confederation of Indian Organisations.

Conrad, P. and Bury, M. (1997) Anslem Strauss and the sociological study of chronic illness: a reflection and appreciation, *Sociology of Health and Illness*, 19(3), 373–82.

Conyard, S., Krishnamurthy, M. and Dosik, H. (1980) Psycho-social aspects of sickle cell anaemia in adolescents, *Health and Social Work*, 5, 20–6.

Corker, M. (1998) *Deaf and Disabled, or Deafness Disabled?* Buckingham: Open University Press.

Crawford, R. (1977) 'You are dangerous to your health': the ideology and politics of victim blaming, *International Journal of Health Services*, 7, 663–80.

Currer, C. and Stacey, M. (eds) (1986) *Concepts of Health, Illness and Disease: A Comparative Perspective*. Leamington Spa: Berg.

Dalley, G. (1988) *Ideologies of Caring: Rethinking Community and Collectivism*. Basingstoke: Macmillan Education.

Darr, Aamra (1990) The social implications of thalassaemia among Muslims of Pakistani origin in England, unpublished doctoral thesis, University of London.

Darr, Aamra and Modell, A. (1988) The frequency of consanguineous marriages among British Pakistanis, *Journal of Medical Genetics*, 25, 186–90.

Darr, Aliya, Jones, L., Ahmad, W.I.U. and Nisar, G. (1997) *A Directory of Initiatives on Ethnicity and Deafness*. York and Bradford: Social Policy Research Unit, York University, and Ethnicity and Social Policy Research Unit, University of Bradford.

Davies, S., Modell, B. and Wonke, B. (1993) The haemoglobinopathies: impact upon black and ethnic minority people, in A. Hopkins and V. Bahl (eds) *Access to Health Care for People from Black and Ethnic Minorities*. London: Royal College of Physicians.

Davis, J.K. and Wasserman, E. (1992) Behavioural aspects of asthma in children, *Clinical Paediatrics*, November, 678–81.

Davison, C. (1997) Everyday ideas of inheritance and health in Britain: implications for predictive genetic testing, in A. Clarke and E. Parsons (eds) *Culture, Kinship and Genes: Towards Cross-Cultural Genetics*. Basingstoke: Macmillan.

Department of Health and Social Security (DHSS) (1986) *Neighbourhood Nursing: A Focus for Care* (The Cumberledge Report). London: DHSS.

Dornbusch, S.M., Patersen, A.C. and Hetherington, E.M. (1991) Projecting the future of research on adolescence, *Journal of Research on Adolescence*, 1, 7–17.

Doyal, L. and Pennel, I. (1979) *The Political Economy of Health*. London: Pluto.

Drury, B. (1991) Sikh girls and the maintenance of an ethnic identity, *New Community*, 17(3), 387–99.

Dyson, S. (1997) Knowledge of sickle cell in a screened population, *Health and Social Care in the Community*, 5(2), 84–93.

Dyson, S.M. (1998) Race, ethnicity and haemoglobin disorders, *Social Science and Medicine*, 47(1), 121–31.

Ebata, A. and Moss, T. (1991) Coping and adjustment in distressed and healthy adolescents, *Journal of Applied Developmental Psychology*, 12, 33–54.

Ehrenreich, J. (1978) *The Cultural Crisis of Modern Medicine*. London and New York: Monthly Review Press.

Eiser, C. (1990) *Chronic Childhood Disease: An Introduction to Psychological Theory and Research*. Cambridge: Cambridge University Press.

Fatimilehin, I.A. and Nadirshaw, Z. (1994) A cross-cultural study of parental attitudes and beliefs about learning disability (mental handicap), *Mental Handicap Research*, 7(3), 202–27.

Fenton, S. (1987) *Ageing Minorities: Black People as They Grow Old in Britain*. London: Commission for Racial Equality.

Finch, J. and Groves, D. (1980) Community care and the family, *Journal of Social Policy*, 9(4), 487–512.

Finch, J. and Mason, J. (1993) *Negotiating Family Responsibilities*. London: Routledge.

Finklestein, V. (1993) Disability: a social challenge or an administrative responsibility?, in J. Swain, V. Finklestein, S. French and M. Oliver (eds) *Disabling Barriers – Enabling Environments*. London: Sage/The Open University.

Ford, J. and Sinclaire, R. (1987) *Sixty Years On: Women Talk about Old Age*. London: Women's Press.

Frydenberg, E. (1997) *Adolescent Coping: Theoretical and Research Perspectives*. London: Routledge.

Fuggle, P., Shand, P.A.X., Gill, L.J. and Davies, S.C. (1996) Pain, quality of life and coping in sickle cell disease, *Archives of Disease in Childhood*, 75, 199–203.

Geiss, S.K., Hobbs, S.A., Hammersley-Maercklein, G., Kramer, J.C. and Henley, M. (1992) Psycho-social factors related to perceived compliance with cystic fibrosis treatment, *Journal of Clinical Psychology*, 48(1), 99–103.

Gilroy, P. (1992) The end of antiracism, in P. Braham, A. Rattansi and R. Skellington (eds) *Racism and Antiracism: Inequalities, Opportunities and Policies*. London: Sage/The Open University.

Goffman, E. (1963) *Stigma: Some Notes on the Management of Spoiled Identity*. Harmondsworth: Penguin.

Green, J.M. (1992) Principles and practicalities of carrier screening: attitudes of recent parents, *Journal of Medical Genetics*, 29, 313–19.

Green, J.M. and France-Dawson, M. (1994) Women's experiences of screening in pregnancy: ethnic differences in the West Midlands. Paper presented to the conference Culture, Kinship and Genes, Institute of Medical Genetics, University of Wales, Abergavenny, 28–30 March.

Green, J.M. and Murton, F.E. (1996) Diagnosis of Duchenne muscular dystrophy: parents' experiences and satisfaction, *Child: Care, Health and Development*, 22(2), 113–28.

Gubrium, J.F. and Sliverman, D. (1989) *The Politics of Field Research: Sociology beyond Enlightenment*. London: Sage.

Harris, J. (1995) *The Cultural Meaning of Deafness: Language, Identity and Power Relations*. Aldershot: Avebury.

Hayford, J.R. and Ross, C.K. (1988) Medical compliance with juvenile rheumatoid arthritis, *Arthritis Care and Research*, 1, 190–7.

Health Education Authority (1998) *Sickle Cell and Thalassaemia: Achieving Health Gain*. London: Health Education Authority.

Henley, A. (1986) Nursing care in a multi-racial society, *Senior Nurse*, 4(2), 18–20.

Herzlich, C. (1973) *Health and Illness: A Social Psychological Analysis*. London: Academic Press.

Hill, M. (1994) 'They are not our brothers': the disability movement and the black disability movement, in N. Begum, M. Hill and A. Stevens (eds) *Reflections: The Views of Black Disabled People on their Lives and Community Care*. London: Central Council for Education and Training in Social Work.

Hill, S.A. (1994) *Managing Sickle Cell Disease in Low Income Families*. Philadelphia, PA: Temple University Press.

Hoare, P. and Mann, H. (1994) Self-esteem and behavioural adjustment in children with epilepsy and children with diabetes, *Journal of Psychosomatic Research*, 38(8), 859–69.

Horowitz, A. (1985) Sons and daughters as caregivers to older parents: differences in role performance and consequences, *The Gerontologist*, 25(6), 612–17.

Hurtig, A.L. (1994) Relationships in families of children and adolescents with sickle cell disease, in K.B. Nash (ed.) *Psycho-social Aspects of Sickle Cell Disease: Past, Present and Future Directions of Research*. New York: Haworth Press.

Hurtig, A.L. and White, L.S. (1986) Psycho-social adjustment in children and adolescents with sickle cell disease, *Journal of Paediatric Psychology*, 11, 411–28.

Hussain, Z. (1997) The Asian community also cares? Informal care given by Asian carers for an individual with a psychiatric illness. MSc. dissertation, University of Leicester.

International Planned Parenthood Federation (1992) *Adolescent Sexual and Reproductive Health*. Paris: Centre International de l'Enfant.

Johnson, S.B. (1988) Psychological aspects of childhood diabetes, *Journal of Child Psychology and Psychiatry*, 29, 729–38.

Joly, D. (1987) Associations among Pakistani population in Britain, in J. Rex and D. Joly with C. Wilpert (eds) *Immigrant Associations in Europe*. Aldershot: Gower.

Jones, L. and Pullen, G. (1995) *Everything You Wanted to Know about Deafness But Did Not Know How to Ask: Doing Research with Deaf People*. York: Joseph Rowntree Foundation (video).

Kalyanpur, M. (1996) The influence of western special education on community-based services in India, *Disability and Society*, 11(2), 249–70.

Katbamna, S. and Bhakta, P., with Parker, G., Ahmad, W.I.U. and Baker, R. (1998) *Experiences and Needs of Carers from the South Asian Communities*, working paper no. 62. Leicester: Nuffield Community Care Studies Unit, University of Leicester.

Katbamna, S., Bhakta, P., Parker, G. and Ahmad, W. (1997) *The Needs of Asian Carers: A Selective Literature Review*, working paper no. 50. Leicester: Nuffield Community Care Studies Unit, University of Leicester.

Kliewer, K. and Lewis, H. (1995) Family influences on coping processes in children and adolescents with sickle cell disease, *Journal of Paediatric Psychology*, 20(4), 511–25.

Klinnert, M.D. (1997) Psycho-social influences on asthma among inner-city children, *Paediatric Pulmonology*, 24, 234–6.

Kreps, G.L. and Kunimoto, E.N. (1994) *Effective Communication in Multicultural Health Care Settings*. Thousand Oaks, CA: Sage.

Lamb, A. (1977) *Primary Health Nursing*. London: Baillière Tindall.

Lamb, B. and Layzell, S. (1994) *Disabled in Britain: A World Apart*. London: Scope.

Lamb, B. and Layzell, S. (1995) *Disabled in Britain: Behind Closed Doors*. London: Scope.

Land, H. and Rose, H. (1985) Compulsory altruism for some or an altruistic society for all, in P. Bean, J. Ferris and D. Whynes (eds) *Defence of Welfare*. London: Tavistock.

Lane, H. (1993) *The Mask of Benevolence: Disabling the Deaf Community*. New York: Random House.

Lane, H., Hoffmeisler, R. and Brahan, B. (1996) *A Journey into the Deaf World*. San Diego, CA: Dawn Sign Press.

Lawrence, M. (1992) Caring for the future, *British Medical Journal*, 305: 400–2.

Lemanek, K.L. (1990) Adherence issues in the medical management of asthma, *Journal of Pediatric Psychology*, 15, 437–58.

Lenney, W., Wells, N.E.J. and O'Neill, B.A. (1994) Burden of paediatric asthma, *European Respiratory Review*, 4(18), 49–62.

Levin, E., Sinclair, I. and Gorbach, P. (1989) *Families, Services and Confusion in Old Age*. Aldershot: Gower.

Lewis, J. and Meredith, B. (1988) *Daughters Who Care*. London: Routledge.

Lipsky, M. (1980) *Street Level Bureaucracy: Dilemmas of the Individual in Public Service*. New York: Russell Sage.

Littlewood, J. (1995) *Current Issues in Community Nursing: Primary Care in Practice*. London: Churchill Livingstone.

Littlewood, R. and Lipsedge, M. (1989) *Aliens and Alienists: Ethnic Minorities and Psychiatry*, 2nd edn. London: Unwin Hyman.

Locker, D. (1997) Living with a chronic illness, in G. Scamber (ed.) *Sociology as Applied to Medicine*. London: W.B. Saunders.

Lonsdale, S. (1990) *Women and Disability: The Experience of Physical Disability among Women*. London: Macmillan.

McCalman, J.A. (1990) *The Forgotten People: Carers in Three Minority Ethnic Communities in Southwark*. London: King's Fund Institute.

Macintyre, S. (1977) *Single and Pregnant*. London: Croom Helm.

Macleur, T.W. (1980) Inbreeding and human fetal death, in I.H. Porter and E.B. Hook (eds) *Human Embryonic and Fetal Death*. New York: Academic Press.

McNaught, A. (1986) *Health Action and Ethnic Minorities*. London: Bedford Square Press.

Mador, J.A. and Smith, D.H. (1989) The psychological adaptation of adolescents with cystic-fibrosis: the review of the literature, *Journal of Adolescent Health Care*, 10(2), 136–42.

Maxwell, K. and Streetly, A. (1998) *Living with Sickle Pain*. London: Department of Public Health Sciences, King's and St Thomas' School of Medicine.

Midence, K. (1994) The effects of chronic illness on children, *Genetic, Social and General Psychology Monographs*, 120(3), 311–26.

Midence, K. and Elander, J. (1994) *Sickle Cell Disease: A Psychosocial Approach*. Oxford: Radcliffe.

Midence, K. and Elander, J. (1996) Adjustment and coping in adults with sickle cell disease: an assessment of research evidence, *British Journal of Health Psychology*, 1, 95–111.

Midence, K., McManus, C., Fuggle, P. and Davies, S. (1996) Psychological adjustment and family functioning in a group of British children with sickle cell disease: preliminary empirical findings and a meta-analysis, *British Journal of Clinical Psychology*, 35, 439–50.

Miller, B. (1987) Gender and control among spouses of the cognitively impaired: a research note, *The Gerontologist*, 27, 447–53.

Minuchin, P. (1974) Families and individual development: provocations from the field of family therapy, *Child Development*, 56, 289–302.

Mishler, E.G. (1986) *Research Interviewing: Context and Narrative*. Cambridge, MA: Harvard University Press.

Modell, B. and Anionwu, E. (1996) Guidelines for screening for haemoglobin disorders: service specifications for low- and high-prevalence DHAs, in W.I.U. Ahmad, T. Sheldon and O. Stuart (eds) *Ethnicity and Health: Reviews of Literature and Guidance for Purchasers in the Areas of Cardiovascular Disease, Mental Health and Haemoglobinopathies*. York: Centre for Reviews and Dissemination and Social Policy Research Unit.

Modood, T. (1988) 'Black' racial equality and Asian identity, *New Community*, 14(3), 397–404.

Modood, T. (1994) *Racial Equality: Colour, Culture and Justice*. London: Institute for Public Policy Research.

Modood, T., Beishon, S. and Virdee, S. (1994) *Changing Ethnic Identities*. London: Policy Studies Institute.

Modood, T., Berthoud, R., Lakey, J., Nazroo, J., Smith, P., Virdee, S. and Beishon, S. (1997) *Ethnic Minorities in Britain: Diversity and Disadvantage*. London: Policy Studies Institute.

Moffat, F. (1996) *London Borough of Sutton GP/Carers Project: Raising the Profile of Carers in General Practice and Primary Care*. London: Wandsworth Health Authority.

Morris, J. (ed.) (1989) *Able Lives: Women's Experience of Paralysis*. London: Women's Press.

Morris, J. (1991) *Pride against Prejudice: Transforming Attitudes to Disability*. London: Women's Press.

Morris, J. (1993) *Community Care or Independent Living*? York: Joseph Rowntree Foundation.

Murray, N. and May, A. (1988) Painful crises in sickle cell disease – patients' perspectives, *British Medical Journal*, 297, 452–4.

Nolan, M., Grant, G. and Keady, J. (1996) *Understanding Family Care*. Buckingham: Open University Press.

Office for National Statistics (ONS) (1996) *Social Focus on Ethnic Minorities*. London: HMSO.

Oliver, M. (1990) *The Politics of Disablement*. London: Macmillan.

Oliver, M. (1993) Re-defining disability: a challenge to research, in J. Swain, V. Finklestein, S. French and M. Oliver (eds) *Disabling Barriers – Enabling Environments*. London: Sage/The Open University.

Oliver, M. (1996) *Understanding Disability: From Theory to Practice*. London: Macmillan.

Opie, A. (1992) *There's Nobody There: Community Care of Confused Older People*. Auckland, NZ and Oxford: Oxford University Press.

Parker, G. (1993a) A four-way stretch? The politics of disability and caring, in J. Swain, V. Finklestein, S. French and M. Oliver (eds) *Disabling Barriers – Enabling Environments*. London: Sage/The Open University.

Parker, G. (1993b) *With This Body: Caring and Disability in Marriage*. Buckingham: Open University Press.

Parker, G. and Lawton, D. (1992) *Different Types of Care, Different Types of Carers*. London: HMSO.

Parker, R. (1981) Tending and social policy, in E.M. Goldberg and S. Hatch (eds) *A New Look at the Personal Social Services*, discussion paper 4. London: Policy Studies Institute.

Parsons, E. and Atkinson, P. (1992) Lay constructions of genetic risk, *Sociology of Health and Illness*, 14, 246–59.

Pearson, M. (1986) Racist notions of ethnicity and culture in health education, in S. Rodmell and A. Watt (eds) *The Politics of Health Education*. London: Tavistock.

Pearson, P. (1992) Defining the primary health care team, *Health Visitor*, 65(10), 358–61.

Pendleton, D. and Hasler, J. (1992) *Doctor–Patient Communication*. London: Academic Press.

Proctor, S.R. and Smith, I.J. (1992) A reconsideration of the factors affecting birth outcome in Pakistani Muslim families in Britain, *Midwifery*, 8, 76–81.

Proctor, S. and Smith, I. (1997) Factors associated with birth outcome in Bradford Pakistanis, in A. Clarke and E. Parsons (eds) *Culture, Kinship and Genes: Towards Cross-cultural Genetics*. Basingstoke: Macmillan.

Prout, A., Hayes, L. and Gelder, L. (1999) Medicines and the maintenance of orderliness in the household management of childhood asthma, *Sociology of Health and Illness*, 21(2), 137–62.

Quine, L. and Pahl, J. (1995) Examining the causes of stress in families with severely mentally handicapped children, *British Journal of Social Work*, 15, 501–17.

Qureshi, H. and Walker, A. (1989) *The Caring Relationship: Elderly People and their Families*. Basingstoke: Macmillan Education.

Rapp, R. (1988) Chromosomes and communication: the discourse of genetic counselling, *Medical Anthropology Quarterly*, 2, 143–57.

Ratcliffe, P. (1996) *'Race' and Housing in Bradford: Addressing the Needs of South Asian, African and Caribbean Communities*. Bradford: Bradford Housing Forum.

Rex, J. (1991) *Ethnic Identity and Ethnic Mobilisation in Britain*. Warwick: Centre for Research in Ethnic Relations.

Said, E. (1978) *Orientalism*. Harmondsworth: Penguin.

Samad, Y. (1992) Book burning and race relations: political mobilisation of Bradford Muslims, *New Community*, 18(4), 507–20.

Schott, J. and Henley, A. (1996) *Culture, Religion and Childbearing in a Multiracial Society: A Handbook for Health Professionals*. Oxford: Butterworth-Heinemann.

Scully, D. and Bart, P. (1978) A funny thing happened to me on the way to the orifice: women in gynaecology textbooks, in J. Ehrenreich (ed.) *The Cultural Crisis of Modern Medicine*. London and New York: Monthly Review Press.

Shackle, D. and May, A. (1989) Knowledge and perceptions of haemoglobinopathy carrier screening among general practitioners in Cardiff, *Journal of Medical Genetics*, 26, 109–12.

Shah, R. (1992) *The Silent Minority: Children with Disabilities in Asian Families*. London: National Children's Bureau.

Sharma, A. and Love, D. (1991) *A Change in Approach: A Report on the Experience of Deaf People from Black and Ethnic Minority Communities*. London: Royal Association in Aid of Deaf People.

Shepperdson, B. (1988) *Growing Up with Down's Syndrome*. London: Cassell.

Sinnema, G. (1992) Youths with chronic illness and disability on their way to social and economic participation: a health care perspective, *Journal of Adolescent Health*, 13, 369–71.

Skellington, R. (1992) *'Race' in Britain Today*. London: Sage.

Sloper, P. and Turner, S. (1992) Service needs of families of children with severe physical disability. *Child: Care, Health and Development*, 18, 259–82.

Social Services Inspectorate (1994a) *Children in Need: Report of Issues Arising from Regional Social Services Inspectorate Workshops*. London: Department of Health.

Social Services Inspectorate (1994b) *Services to Disabled Children and their Families*. London: HMSO.

Standing Medical Advisory Committee (SMAC) (1994) *Report of Working Party on Sickle Cell, Thalassaemia and Other Haemoglobinopathies*. London: Department of Health.

Stark, L.J., Dahlquist, L.M. and Collins, F.L. (1987) Improving children's compliance with diabetes management, *Clinical Psychology Review*, 7, 223–42.

Stimmel, B. (1993) *Pain Analgesia and Addiction*. New York: Raven Press.

Strunk, R.C., Mrazek, D.A., Fuhrmann, G.S.W. and LaBrecque, J.F. (1985) Physiologic and psychological characteristics associated with deaths due to asthma in childhood: a case-controlled study, *Journal of the American Medical Association*, 254, 1193–8.

Stuart, O. (1996) 'Yes, we mean black disabled people too': thoughts on community care and disabled people from black and minority ethnic communities, in W.I.U. Ahmad and K. Atkin (eds) *'Race' and Community Care*. Buckingham: Open University Press.

Stubblefield, H.W. (1977) Religion, parents and mental retardation, in C.J. Drew, M.L. Hardman and H.P. Bluhm (eds) *Mental Retardation: Social and Educational Perspectives*. St Louis, MO: C.V. Mosby.

Swain, J., Finklestein, V., French, S. and Oliver, M. (eds) (1993) *Disabling Barriers – Enabling Environments*. London: Sage/The Open University.

Thompson, R.J. (1994) Stability and change in psychological adjustments of mothers of children and adolescents with cystic fibrosis and sickle cell disease, *Journal of Paediatric Psychology*, 19(2), 171–88.

Tomlin, Z. (1994) Lost for words, *Health Service Journal*, 25 August: 12.

Turner, B.S. (1987) *Medical Power and Social Knowledge*. London: Sage.

Turner, P. and Sloper, P. (1992) Paediatrician's disclosure and follow-up of severe physical disability in young children, *Developmental Medicine and Clinical Neurology*, 34, 348–58.

Twigg, J. (1989) Models of carers: how do social care agencies conceptualize their relationship with informal carers?, *Journal of Social Policy*, 18(1), 53–66.

Twigg, J. and Atkin, K. (1994) *Carers Perceived*. Buckingham: Open University Press.

Walco, G.A. and Dampier, C.D. (1990) Pain in children and adolescents with sickle cell disease: a descriptive study, *Journal of Paediatric Psychology*, 15(5), 643.

Walker, R. and Ahmad, W.I.U. (1994) Windows of opportunity in rotting frames: care providers' perspectives on community care and black communities, *Critical Social Policy*, 40, 46–69.

Walmsley, A. (1993) Contradiction in caring: reciprocity and interdependence, *Disability, Handicap and Society*, 2, 129–41.

Ward, L. (1990) Blinded by the light, *Community Care*, 9 July.

Watson, E. (1984) Health of infants and use of health services by mothers of different ethnic groups in East London, *Community Medicine*, 6, 127–35.

Webb-Johnson, A. (1991) *A Cry for Change: An Asian Perspective on Developing Quality Mental Health Care*. London: Confederation of Indian Organisations.

Westwood, S. and Bhachu, P. (eds) (1988) *Enterprising Women: Economy and Gender Relations*. London: Routledge.

Whitten, C.F. and Fischoff, J. (1974) Psycho-social effects of sickle cell disease, *Archives of Internal Medicine*, 133, 681–9.

Wiles, R. and Robinson, J. (1994) Teamwork in primary care: the views and experiences of nurses, midwives and health visitors, *Journal of Advanced Nursing*, 20, 324–30.

Williams, R. (1993) Religion and illness, in A. Radley (ed.) *Worlds of Illness: Biographical and Cultural Perspectives on Health and Disease*. London: Routledge.

World Health Organization (WHO) (1989) *The Health of Youth*. Geneva: World Health Organization.

Wright, C. (1983) Language and communication problems in an Asian community, *Journal of the Royal College of General Practitioners*, 33, 101–4.

Yee, L. (1995) *Improving Support for Black Carers: A Source-Book of Information, Ideas and Service Initiatives*. London: King's Fund Institute.

Index